The Ride Along

Guilty Until She Proves Otherwise

By Gerald C. Anderson, Sr.

ISBN: 978-1-957333-05-2

Lyfe Publishing

Publishers Since 2012

Published by Lyfe Publishing LLC

Lyfe Publishing, 10800 Nautica Place, White Plains MD 20695

Copyright © 2022 by Gerald C. Anderson, Sr.

Library of Congress Cataloging in Publications Data

Gerald C. Anderson, Sr.

The Ride Along / Gerald C. Anderson, Sr.

ISBN: 978-1-957333-05-2

(Fictitious Character)-Fiction

1. Washington DC
2. The Ride Along–Fiction

Printed in the United States of America

1 2 3 4 5 6 7 8 9 10

Book design by Olivia Pro Designs and Lyfe Designs

Editors

Beryl Anthony Brackett

Chief Editor

BAB Productions, LLC

18103 Merino Drive

Accokeek, Maryland 20607

Reviewers

Danny Sells

Lahla-Hadiya Castro

DEDICATION

Back in the mid 90's, I met a black female law enforcement officer. During that time, I got to watch her in action as she patrolled the base where I was stationed. Although she was never in a situation such as the one depicted in *The Ride Along,* she inspired me to write this novel.

Being raised by a number of black females in my family imprinted upon me the strength of our women. They are loving, caring and despite the situation, they can maintain their own in a struggle.

I dedicate this novel to all the black female women I know. Thank you for your strength, courage and kindness. You have endured many trials, yet you continue to move forward. Without you, the black man would be nothing.

Also, By Gerald C. Anderson, Sr.

ACKNOWLEDGEMENT

THANK YOU FOR YOUR SUPPORT WITH "THE RIDE ALONG"

Beryl Brackett

Danny Sells

Lahla-Hadiya Castro

Prologue

Blade Samuels stood in front of the five gang leaders in East City. For years, the gangs ran parts of the city and fought over territory. Today, things would change. He cleared his throat to get their attention, "Gentlemen, it's time for the fighting and bickering over territory to stop. The time has to come for us to come together and control this city as one united unit; focus on money, power, and control. That's what the government has done for years, not to mention that's what the police fear most; a united criminal force. If we take this step, we will all be rich and unstoppable."

Armando Sessions ran the Black Knights. He stood and replied, "So, we are to hand over our hard earned territory and money to you to run. We have fought for years to gain and control what we have." He laughed and looked around the room, "My family has run The Black Knights for over 20 years. Now, you say we should simply hand it over to you and all will be okay. You say all of us will be rich and powerful? I'm already rich and powerful."

Blade hated short-sighted people, especially those who did not buy into his vision of a united gang to rule East City. He snickered and walked over to Armando. "Armando, my friend, I remember when you started your career. You struggled to build any kind of a name, but I recognized your strength. I backed your moves when your fellow Knights didn't believe in you. Now, you question my vision? Now you think you can lead this entire city? Really?"

Armando took a stance. "I may have struggled to start my leadership, but it's not about how you start my friend. It's about where you finish. I rose to be the leader of the Black Knights faster than anyone in history. It's no accident. I know how to run a gang and I could run this city better than anyone. That includes you… my friend."

Blade was becoming very annoyed. He discussed his plan with each leader before this meeting and they all agreed with his idea. Even Armando agreed, but now he's making a power play in front of the rest of the group. This was not good. Blade needed to send a message. One the group would always remember. It's good he prepared.

Blade nodded his head. He looked at Armando's lieutenant, then placed his large hands on each of Armando's shoulders. "This is how you treat an old friend? Just the other day, we were all in agreement. Now you make a play like this?" Blade popped his lips and with a quickness not seen by anyone in the room before he spun Armando around and snapped his neck like a toothpick.

The sound echoed through the quiet room. The other four leadership shifted the weight in their seats, each not wanting the other to see how uncomfortable they were. Blade stared at each of them one-by-one. His eyes rested on Carlos. He said, "Carlos, you are now the leader of the Black Knights. Do you question my vision?"

Carlos shook his head, "I do not."

"Good." He looked at the remaining leaders, "Does anyone else question my vision?" The room was silent. His message was clear, and no one would question him again.

Chapter 1

Twanda Cousins hailed from Tampa, Florida. She grew up off of 22nd Street in the projects everyone knew as Belmont Heights. She loved her hometown and her hood but life called her to another level. She scored higher than anyone in her neighborhood on her SATs and got into East City University. After high school she moved to East City. She wanted to get ahead in life and return some day to help others find a way out.

She sat in her science class daydreaming about her mother. She missed her more than anything. Her mom was 49 when she got pregnant with her only child, Twanda. Her father told her about the excitement they had when her mom found out she was pregnant.

Twanda often talked to her dad about the pregnancy. She wondered why they went through with it when the probability of her mom surviving was low. Listening to her professor talk about the science of procreation bothered her. Her mother gave her life so Twanda could live.

Twanda had to run across campus to get to her next last class. He car broke down the day before. Tired and out of breath she rested in front of the Criminal Justice building. "Hey, Twanda, you tired?"

She looked at him with her eyes crossed. "Why are you in my space Melvin?" She gathered her books and walked inside the building.

"Hey, don't be mad at me. I didn't break your car."

"No you didn't, but you won't stop teasing me about it either. Again, why are you in my space?"

"Okay, I won't say another word. You ready for this quiz?"

"I was born ready. That's why I have an A in this class, remember?"

Melvin sighed, "Who doesn't remember? You have an A in every class."

They entered the classroom and took their seats. Twanda always sat at the front of the room. She never wanted to miss any instruction given by her professors. Melvin asked, "Are you still going on that ride along tomorrow night?"

"Yes, sir! I can't wait to go. I've seen the police all the time in the projects. This will be a chance to actually see them work."

"Hey you might be part of shooting. Hopefully, it won't be another black man."

Twanda sighed and popped her lips, "Why do I hang with you?"

"Because I'm cool."

She laughed, "If you say so."

Professor Lawrence walked in and stood in front of the class. He started, "Welcome students. As you get ready for your last days at East City University you should be aware of a major shift in power in the city. Word has come out that the gangs in the city have united into one unit. Anyone know what this could mean for our city's police force?" Twanda raised her hand. Professor Lawrence replied, "My star student, Twanda Cousins."

"The uniting of the gangs in the city will make it nearly impossible for the police to make arrest. In the past they would pit the gangs against each other to get information and use that information to make arrest. Now this might be impossible."

"You are correct as usual young lady. You will make a fine law enforcement officer or dare I say it, lawyer." The class laughed knowing Professor Lawrence despised lawyers.

Melvin replied, "Yes, she will." The class broke out in more laughter.

Professor Lawrence continued, "Then there is Mr. Melvin Goings. Mr. Goings, are you ready for your quiz today? Your grade can use some help." The class laughed even louder and Melvin slid down in his seat.

The quiz went as Twanda expected. She whizzed through it and hit the door. She loved quizzes in Professor Lawrence's class because the sooner she finished the sooner she could leave.

It was time to put in some work at the gym. Twanda had to stay in shape. Her basketball career may end with her senior year in college, but she knew she had to stay in shape for the FBI Academy. Her martial arts training needed some tune up as well. She had not been to the gym in a week, but hearing the comments flowing into her ears from the men she passed on her way to the gym confirmed she still looked good.

She pushed open the gym door and walked onto the court. One of the men's basketball players said, "Twanda, you want me to school you today?"

She stopped and placed her hands on her hips in ghetto fashion, popped her lips to say, "Don't you wish you could?"

Ralph laughed, "Come guys, I got Twanda, so you're done." He looked at Twanda and grinned, "That look… goodness, you must be from the hood."

"Born and raised. I'm not ashamed at all."

The game began, and Twanda held her own with the guys. Her team won. After the game Ralph said, "You're still dating that dude?"

"Yep, hopefully we'll get married someday."

Ralph popped his lips, "Come on T, you and I could light up the world. We're both star basketball players and in top shape. We look better than any couple around."

"Ralph, how many times have we had this conversation? We're friends and that's all we will ever be. Kenyon and I are a great couple. Do I wish he would work out more with me? I do, but I love him for the man that he is and not for the man I want him to be."

"Understood. Want to hit the treadmill?"

"Yeah, then some weights and I'm out of here. I got a big date tonight."

"I don't want to hear it." They laughed and Twanda finished her workout. After her workout with Ralph, Twanda rushed over to her dorm room and cleaned up. She had a date with her boyfriend, Kenyon, and she was looking forward to it.

Kenyon and Twanda started dating in their freshmen year. She loved him because he had a plan for his life and set out to execute it. She admired men who knew what they wanted and went for it. The best part of his plan was that it included her. When he told her he loved her despite her commitment to not having sex until she was married, she smiled and never stopped. Tonight, she believed he would ask her to marry him. She wondered if she would say 'yes' immediately or make him wait. She had not decided yet.

After she showered and dressed, she called her dad. Wilson Cousins was in an assisted living home. Twanda was born when he was 53 years old. Now, with his failing health, he needed around the clock care. Twanda wanted to be there, but he encouraged her to get her degree and become the FBI agent she wanted to become.

"Hi dad, how are you today?"

"I'm well, baby girl. How are you?"

She sighed, "It's been a tough day. My car is in the shop, but thank God we have an automotive technology department here and I have a couple of friends getting their degrees in that department. Otherwise, I wouldn't be able to afford it."

"Life has some advantages and you shouldn't be ashamed of taking advantage of those that come to you."

"I'm not ashamed, daddy. I'm thankful."

"How's that young man treating you?"

Twanda smiled, "He's treating me very well, daddy. I'm meeting him for dinner tonight." She paused with enthusiasm in her heart, trying to hold in the next sentence, but to no avail. "Dad, I think he's going to pop the question."

"What will be your response?" Wilson was always so cool. Nothing seemed to bother him. Twanda loved that about him and prayed she could be the same way.

"I have not decided if I'm going to say 'yes' immediately or make him wait."

"So it's going to be 'yes' either way?"

Her smiled wore so big on her face those looking could only believe she was excited beyond words. "Yes sir, I'm going to marry him, daddy."

Wilson giggled. She knew he wanted the best for her. With his failing health, he often hoped that good would be Kenyon. "Well, he'd better take care of my little girl. I will not be here forever, so someone needs to step up."

Twanda laughed, "I will bring him to meet you the first chance I get."

"I can't wait to meet him, baby."

"But daddy, I don't need a man to take care of me. You made an athletic girl here and I can fend for myself."

"Baby, both your parents were college athletes, so I know you can take care of yourself. It doesn't hurt to have a man by your side to help you."

"I know daddy."

Wilson continued, "Well, it's time for me to get my dinner. I need to get there before Joe Lodato. He's greedy."

Twanda burst out in laughter, "Daddy, you're too much. I'll call you tomorrow and let you know what Kenyon and I decide."

"Great. Have a great evening, baby girl."

"Thank you, daddy and you too." She hung up the phone, smiling at her conversation with her dad. *"He's the greatest man I know this side of Heaven. Lord, keep him here for as long as possible. I love him so much."* Twanda rushed out the door. The restaurant was five blocks from campus, so she did not need her car to get there. The exercise was good for her. After her basketball career ended, she had not exercised as much. Getting ready for graduation got in the way. She planned to increase her gym time more after Quantico.

Twanda arrived at the restaurant. Kenyon stood waiting for her with that all too familiar grin on his face. "Hi sweetheart, I hope I didn't make you wait too long."

"Hey, Twanda, and no you didn't. Waiting for you is an honor, not a chore."

"Ahh, dude you're off to a great start." The host led them to a comfortable booth at the back of the restaurant. Twanda smiled when she saw the table. "Oh, my! Kenyon, you are going all out tonight, baby."

"Anything for you, my love."

She sniffed the roses and took in their scent. "These look and smell amazing. Thank you, honey." She kissed him on his lips. Her emotions ran deep into her spirit with each second. She didn't want to let go, but the constant clearing of the host's throat told her she needed to. "I'm sorry, but it's not every day that a girl gets roses on her dinner table."

Kenyon said, "It should be." Twanda's smile grew larger. Kenyon continued, "Thank you, Miss. We'll have a glass of Chardonnay."

The server snapped, "Coming right up."

Twanda said, "Sweet compliments, roses and now expensive wine… did you knock over a bank?"

"No baby, remember my plan to be a successful businessman before I'm 30 years old?" She nodded. "Well, I am well on my way. I presented my business plan to 30 investors and guess what?"

"Well, don't leave me hanging?"

"I got $250,000 for my business! Baby, you're looking at the next king of the food truck industry."

"Oh, wow! I'm so proud of you, Kenyon. That's amazing."

Kenyon's smiled disappeared. "There's just one catch."

"Oh Lord what?"

"I need to move to Los Angeles."

His words stabbed her deep in her heart. She expected to be receiving a marriage proposal, not the news that her boyfriend of four years was relocating across the country. "What does that mean for us?"

"I don't know, baby…" The server arrived with the Chardonnay and sat the glasses on the table. Twanda did not take her eyes off of Kenyon. She could not think of the right words to say, but her heart sank deeper by the minute. The server handed her a glass with Chardonnay in it. Kenyon held his glass up, "Can we toast to the future?"

Depressed as she felt, she raised her glass and instantly saw a sparkle that wasn't wine. She shouted, "Oh, my God!" Customers turned and looked to see what the shouting was about. Twanda was a little embarrassed, but not enough to restrain her emotions.

Kenyon stood. More excitement rose inside of Twanda. He took a knee and placed her hand in his. She couldn't stand it any longer. Twanda shouted, "Yes!" Everyone burst into laughter.

Kenyon said, "Baby, I have to ask you first."

"I'm sorry, go ahead."

Kenyon continued, "Baby, you don't have to shake." She nodded, "Since the day I met you, you have inspired me to go to heights I never envisioned for myself. The love you have showed me things I couldn't have imagined. There's no one else in the world I would rather spend the rest of my life with than you." Twanda struggled to keep it inside. "Will you marry me?"

"Yes!" Again she shouted the answer for all to hear and answered her question of earlier in the day. She immediately said 'yes' instead of waiting.

After dinner, Kenyon suggested a walk along the river. The couple strolled along the bank of the Potomac River, a popular hangout this time of evening for couples. Twanda enjoyed every moment with him. She gazed into his eyes and they kissed. Kenyon asked, "So, is moving to L.A. going to be a problem for you?"

"Nope, they have an FBI headquarters there. After Quantico I will ask to be assigned there. Let's pray it all works out."

"Yeah, let's do that. In fact, how about we go to the Pastor tomorrow and talk to him?"

Twanda smiled again. This was a night of smiles for her. Everything was going better than expected. She said, "I have class until noon. After that, I'm down. Oh, and we have to go tell daddy in person."

"I have class until 1, so I'll pick you up in front of your dorm. Then we'll go see the Pastor, then your dad."

"Great, but I have to be back by 9. My ride along is scheduled for 10:30. I'm going to be part of the 11 to 7 shift."

"I'm so against that, but I guess I have to get use to you being out there in dangerous situations."

"Yeah, if I'm going to be an FBI agent, you'll have to get used to it, buddy." The couple laughed and headed back to the campus.

Early the next morning, Twanda rose. Her roommate, Sybil, startled her. "Hey girl, you're just coming in now?"

Sybil replied, "Yeah, I had a date with my boo."

"Oh, goodness."

"How about you? Did you get laid last night?"

Twanda giggled, "You know I'm waiting until marriage, so that would be a no."

"Girl, you better let that man have some before he explodes."

"I got something better last night."

"What?"

"A ring!"

"What! Are you serious? You guys are going to get married?"

"Yes, we are. We are going to talk to our pastor today, then go visit my dad afterwards. I can say it was all worth it."

"Well, I said you were crazy four years ago, but I guess you found the right man to hold out until he marries you. None of my boyfriends would wait."

Twanda snapped her fingers, proud of the God she serves. "When you trust God, you can wait. I can do all things with Him."

"Well, congratulations Miss Christian Girl. You stood in your belief and now you are receiving your reward."

"Actually, my reward is in Heaven but…" She twisted her head and grinned, "Thank you."

"You're too much. Seriously, your life is perfect and I'm sure it will get better from here. Hey, you still doing that ride along tonight?"

"Yeah, I have to be there at 10:30."

"Cool. When I did mine, it was so much fun. The officer was hitting on me, though. I almost gave him some, too."

"Lord have mercy." Twanda walked into the shower to get ready to greet her man. She reminisced about her life and smiled. Sybil was right, to some degree, she had a near perfect life. The water rained down on her. She appreciated the simple things in life, like a nice, warm shower. It did not hurt if it were long, too. In the projects where she was born and raised, they did not have showers. Her family was comprised of her parents and two siblings, both boys. Twanda never had her own room until she was 15 and the boys moved out.

The feeling of loss encapsulated her whenever she thought about her brothers. Both ended up running with gangs and lost their lives early. *Too much death for one family to endure, but I'm going to change all that, Lord. I'm going to be the life bringer.*

Sybil walked back into the room while Twanda got dressed. Twanda said, "Sybil, my life is not perfect. My family has suffered so much death. I just want to live right so I can turn things around."

"I get it. I shouldn't have said that stupid comment. I know your history. I guess I just meant you're doing perfect now."

"Thanks."

"Sometimes I wish I had your strength. Instead, I see a man and want him bad. I can't help myself."

"Come to church with me."

Sybil walked out of the room without responding. Twanda knew that meant she did not want to talk about church. Church was something Sybil and her family avoided since a Catholic priest molested her cousin.

Twanda finished dressing and listened for the knock she became accustomed to hearing. Rat-a-tat-tat two quick times was his signature knock. It brought joy to her heart to hear it. Twanda swung open the door and there he stood; her king. She embraced him, "Good morning, honey! It's nice to see you again."

"Good morning, my queen. It brings me happiness to stare upon your golden face once more."

Sybil returned and brushed between them, "You both suck. Hey, Kenyon. I'll see you later, Twanda."

"Bye, Sybil." Twanda laughed, "Don't mind her, she's jealous of our impending nuptials."

"I get it. Who wouldn't be angry seeing two beautiful people uniting as one?"

"Good one, but I think she's more upset at the fact that we have remained virgins throughout the process."

"Girl, don't say that too loud. My boys might hear."

"Are you serious? You should be proud."

"Look, I wasn't a virgin when I met you, but I knew if anyone was worthy of my being celibate, it would be you. But let's keep that on the down low."

"Let's go before I get angry." They headed out the door and to the church where they attended service each Sunday. Twanda did more than just attend church on Sunday, she ushered as well. She wanted to be involved in the church now because she may not have the opportunity after she became an agent.

They arrived at the church after having few words in the vehicle. Twanda loved him, but she did not like the fact he wanted to hide his celibacy from his friends. She believes it should be a badge of honor, not a secret. Before the pastor arrived, she asked, "Are you ashamed to be celibate for me?"

"No, I'm excited about our future. I can't wait to marry you, Twanda." She stared at him with cold eyes. "Okay, yes, I don't want my friends to know I've gone without sex for four years. I've been the man with ladies, not a punk."

"Oh my God, Kenyon. You should be proud of your accomplishment. Look at where we are today. We're about to be married and we don't know each other in that way." She emphasized, "Not many people can say that." Before he could respond, Pastor Cleveland Jennings joined them. "Hi, Pastor Jennings."

"My favorite young couple is here. It's a pleasure to see you both."

Kenyon replied, "Hi, Pastor Jennings."

"Okay, both of you seem to have something pressing on your hearts. Should we discuss it?"

Twanda answered, "It's not important, Pastor." That was a lie. It was very important to her, but she did not want to hash it out at that point. "We just wanted to come here and let you know we decided to get married."

"That's wonderful news! When is the date?"

Kenyon answered, "We haven't decided on that yet, but I have business that's starting in Los Angeles. We will need to get married sometime in June. Is that okay with you, Twanda?"

"June is fine with me, honey. In fact, it would be a great birthday present for my dad."

Pastor Jennings said, "I love it when everything works out. We can schedule a meeting to go over all the details. We'll also need to do some counselling. Judging from your faces there is something we need to discuss." Twanda and Kenyon did not answer. "Okay, how's next Tuesday at seven in the evening?"

Kenyon answered, "I'm good with it."

Twanda replied, "So am I." She looked at Kenyon, trying not to show any madness. "Thanks, Pastor, we need to get to my dad."

"It was great seeing you both. I hope to see you Sunday."

Kenyon replied, "We'll be there as always."

"Outstanding, drive safe and, Twanda, tell your dad I said 'hello'."

"I will pastor. Thank you."

They walked out of the chapel and headed to the assisted living home where her father stayed. This time of day, he would be on the lawn enjoying the sunshine. Her father was an outdoorsman when he was younger. Wilson Cousins held state and national records in track and field. He loved to run and was proud he passed that gene on to his daughter. Every chance Wilson got, he would go outside. Twanda and Kenyon arrived and found her father sitting in his customary seat in front of the biggest tree on the lawn.

"Hi, daddy!"

He forced himself to his feet and hugged his daughter. She loved the feel of being in her father's arms. It was an experience she knew was coming closer to an end. "My baby girl, it's so good to see you again."

Twanda's heart raced with the feeling his warm embrace brought to her. Her mom passed five years before and now he was all she had. "So, daddy, this is my fiancée, Kenyon. Kenyon, this is my daddy."

"How are you, Mr. Cousins?"

"I'm doing well, son. So you want to marry my baby girl?"

"Yes, sir. She's everything I want and more in a woman."

"Well, that's good to hear. I don't have long for this world and I would like to die knowing my daughter was in the hands of a good man. Is that going to be you, son?"

"Yes, sir. I would cross Heaven and Earth to help her."

Wilson struggled to return to his wheelchair, "Okay, we will see. When is this wedding going to happen?"

Twanda said, "In your birth month, daddy. We're getting married in June."

Wilson smiled at the news, "That's great. I can't wait to be there to give my baby girl away."

The nurse joined them, "Mr. Cousins, it's time to go inside now."

"Well, baby girl, it must be time for me to get some dinner. You come back and see me this weekend so we can talk longer."

"I will, daddy."

"Bring my new son-in-law with you."

"I'll be here, Mr. Cousins."

"Good, I'll see your both later."

Twanda hugged him and the couple returned to Kenyon's vehicle. The drive into East City was quiet. It took them through the area known as Southeast; a place that put Twanda on edge. She heard many stories about things that happened to innocent people driving through the worst part of East City. She imagined what the young woman must have endured when she stopped to get gas, only to be raped by a gang in broad daylight.

They pulled up to a light and two men were standing on the corner. Twanda had enough training in law enforcement and experience growing up in the projects to recognize a drug dealer. She quietly prayed, *"Lord, please let this light change before they notice us."* It didn't.

A black SUV pulled up to the men. A tall, stout man stepped out of the vehicle. Twanda recognized him from the news and reports they reviewed in class. His name was Blade Samuels. He grabbed the man by his throat and said something to him. She could not hear the words, but the actions sent shivers up and down her spine. Kenyon said, "You see that?"

"Run the light."

"What?"

"Run the damn light!"

Kenyon did as she said. "If I get a ticket, you better get me out of it." Twanda did not respond. "You hear me?"

"Yes, Kenyon, I hear you. You don't want to be a witness to any crime that man commits."

"Who is he?"

"He's the worst crime lord East City has ever known. Everyone in law enforcement knows him, but no one can put an end to him. Word has it he has combined all the gangs into one. He will be hard to bring down now."

"Forget about that ticket then, baby."

They pulled onto the campus and Kenyon parked in front of Twanda's dorm. She breathed out a sigh of release. "I have to get used to confronting men like Blade if I'm going to be an FBI agent."

"But then, baby, you'll have a team of agents to help you instead of a food truck businessman." The comment made her giggle. It was nice to laugh about something between them. They spent the day arguing over something that would not matter. "Anyway, baby, I can sit with you until it's time. Is your car fixed?"

"Thanks, I hoped you would. No, my broke down piece of junk isn't fixed yet. Hopefully tomorrow." They walked inside the dorm and into Twanda's room. Sybil sat on her bed. "Hey, Sybil. What's up?"

"Nothing."

"Okay, we both know that's not true. Tell me what's up or I'll have to badger you for the rest of the night." Sybil knew she would do it.

"My brother was found dead an hour ago."

"Oh, no! What happened?"

"Blade happened! Why doesn't anyone put that bastard in jail?"

Twanda sat next to her, "I'm so sorry. Are you going home?"

"My sister is on the way to get me."

Twanda said, "I can go with you. I will reschedule my ride along."

"No, Twanda, don't. You do your ride along. There's nothing you can do at my parents' house. Come by tomorrow. We'll be there. We'll probably have a ton of food. You know how they do in the projects."

"I do know, my friend. Unfortunately, we both have experienced it far too many times." They both acknowledged each other and Sybil left the room. Twanda sat down across from Kenyon. She wondered what was going through his head but hesitated to ask. She did not want another argument.

Kenyon asked, "So this ride along, it's safe, right? They aren't going to put a civilian in danger, right?"

"No, baby. It's a simple ride along on the graveyard shift. I won't be in any danger."

Kenyon popped his lips. "Why the graveyard shift? That's when all the crime is going down. Couldn't they have put you on the day shift?"

"I asked for the graveyard shift."

"I should have known."

Twanda giggled inside. *Just when I didn't want to argue, guess what I get… an argument.* She said, "You know I want to experience life as a law enforcement officer on the street. What better way to learn than to see the most action? At least it's a Thursday night. I could see you whining if it were a Saturday night."

"Whining? Are you serious right now?"

"Mistake." She gasped, "I'm sorry. That came out wrong. I know you're concerned, but I'll be okay. There's an armed officer with me. Nothing can go wrong."

Kenyon sighed, stood and looked deep into Twanda's eyes, "Whenever anyone says there's nothing that can go wrong, that's when all hell breaks loose."

Twanda laughed, "You are such a…" She pulled back on her comment, knowing it would not endear her to him.

"Such a what? Go ahead, finish that sentence."

She smiled and stood with him. She pecked him on the lips. "You're such a sweet and caring soul. I don't know what I would do without you. It's time for me to go." He starred at her. She knew he suspected she lied about the sentence, but it was for his own good. He turned to the door and walked out. Kenyon did not bother to turn around. She thought, *"I guess he might ask for his ring back now."*

Chapter 2

Twanda stood antsy in the back of the briefing room as Bravo shift received their instructions from Sergeant Benson. She could not wait to get out on the streets and see how the officers performed their duties.

Sergeant Benson announced, "As most of you know, we have been doing a ride along program with East City University and tonight we have 4.0 student Twanda Cousins with us." The officers applauded. "Miss Cousins will ride with Diego Ramirez tonight, so Ramirez take care of the civilian. Don't let anything happen to her."

"Yes, sir, boss." Everyone laughed and make jokes at Ramirez's expense.

Sergeant Benson continued, "That's it, everyone. Hit the streets and most of all, be safe out there."

The officers broke out into their groups and several of them greeted Twanda. Officer Ramirez made his way to Twanda. "Miss Cousins, it will be nice to have you riding with me tonight."

"Please call me Twanda. Miss Cousins sounds so… old."

They both laughed, "You got it, Twanda. Come on." He lead her out to the garage where all the vehicles were parked. They got into Officer Ramirez's cruiser. He continued, "Now this is the control center right here. I have my computer where I can run plates, my shotgun if I need it, my speed gun and most of all… my music, yeah! I hope you like rap."

"I do listen to some of it, but nothing that demeans women."

"Oh, I don't listen to that crap. I need to listen to something motivational, you know."

"I do, and I can understand that."

Officer Ramirez pulled out onto the street. "Tonight we're going to check out main street for a while, see how the clubbers are doing, then come around to the beltway and lastly we end up in Southeast. I know some people cringed at Southeast, but that's my spot. My people are there."

"Your people?"

"Yeah, Latinos, Blacks, Mexicans, they're all my people. I love them."

"You're something else, Officer Ramirez."

"Come on now, we're first name here… call me Diego."

"You got it."

Officer Ramirez headed towards main street and the downtown area of East City. Downtown was lit up at night and most of the clubs and bars were busy with customers. Officer Ramirez said, "Now down here you have the good people who are just looking to have a good time, but then you have those who you know are trying to start some trouble. These clubs north of Main Street are good. We usually cruise around and make sure nobody is getting out of hand. For the most part, nothing happens down here except your occasional brawl or something."

"Yeah, I come down here from time to time. I hang out at The Palace because it's clean. Most of the people there are well dressed and mannered."

"Yeah, The Palace is a good spot. I don't think I've had a call there before. The manager is a cool dude too. He don't take no mess."

"So, do you build up relationships with the community?"

"I do, but I can't speak for all my fellow officers. Some of them, well, you know they think they're better than people. I believe in serving the people."

"Is this your wife and kids?"

"Oh, yeah. They are my reason for living. Me and my wife been married for 10 years. Juan is 8 and Luiz is 4. Love my boys."

Twanda smiled at the picture. "They're little handsome men."

"Thank you. How about you? Are you married?"

"No, not yet. I'm supposed to get married in June, but my fiancée might change his mind after tonight."

"Ah, it will blow over. If he's a smart man, he'll go through with the wedding." Officer Ramirez pulled over. He looked down the alley where two men were standing facing each other. "Now we have some action. Stay here."

"Okay."

Officer Ramirez got out of the vehicle and walked over to the men. He had his hand on his gun. Twanda heard him call out to the men. They both raised their hands.

After a brief conversation, the men lowered their hands and walked away. Officer Ramirez returned to the cruiser. "False alarm. Just two guys looking to hook up with each other."

"Male prostitution?"

"No, apparently they met in the club and fell out with each other. Lover's quarrel is more like it."

"That's so nasty."

"Tell me about it. God didn't make us to date the same gender."

"You're a church going man?"

"I should be. I slacked off and haven't been to church in a while, but it's still in me. How about you?"

"I'm a diehard Christian. I love the Lord."

"Good, we need more young people like you."

A call came over the radio, "Charlie-23, we have a 10-15 at 4211 Roscoe Road. Be advised the perpetrates may be armed."

"Roger that. Charlie-23 responding."

Twanda said, "10-15 is a civil disturbance, right?"

"That's right and they're armed, so you need to stay in the vehicle."

"I got it. Can't put the civilian in harm's way." She giggled, "One day I'm going to be one kicking down doors."

"It's my job to keep you alive until that day, Twanda."

"Ah thank you, Diego." Diego asked, "Do you want to cut the lights on?"

Twanda giggled at the thought, "I guess everyone wants to do that, right?" Diego nodded. "Yeah, let me turn them on." She pushed the button to start the siren and lights. Twanda felt a thrill throughout her body. "I can't believe how good that felt."

Diego laughed. "Everyone gets that when they turn them on for the first time."

The cruiser pulled up to the resident. Several people stood outside and Twanda heard shouting from inside the house. She asked, "Can I stand outside with the rest of the onlookers?"

"Sure, that should be okay. Just don't get hurt."

She laughed, "I will do my best."

Officer Ramirez got out of the vehicle and headed to the door of the residence. Twanda watched from the sidewalk with everyone else. Most people were speculating on what was going on inside. She heard a woman say, "He's always beating on her. They need to take him to jail."

Another person replied, "They have and she just bails him out. He's right in the house the next day. Honestly, I don't know why the police respond. It's a waste of time."

Twanda listened to the back and forth. She wanted to comment, but thought it best to remain anonymous. Other patrol cars pulled up as the man shouted at Officer Ramirez. Twanda worried that something would happen to him. Her fears were soon realized.

The man burst out the door with a tire iron in hand. He swung it at Officer Ramirez but missed. The other officers pulled out their weapons and shouted at the man. The man was in a rage. He did not respond to the officer's request to put his weapon down. Officer Ramirez dodged the next swing and grabbed the man. The two men went to the ground.

The other officers jumped on the man and together they wrestled with him and handcuffed him. He shouted profanities at the officers as they hauled him into one of the cruisers.

Officer Ramirez brushed himself off and called out, "Hey Twanda, come over here."

Twanda felt special as she made her way out of the group of onlookers. She heard them talking about her. Some were good, and some were bad. Officer Ramirez said, "You sure you want this life?" The officers all laughed.

Officer Baker chimed in, "She wants to be an FBI agent, so she won't have to deal with scum like this." They all laughed again.

Twanda said, "Come on now, the FBI has its dangerous criminals too, guys."

Officer Wilson added, "Twanda, don't listen to these guys. As women, we have to set the mark higher. They're just jealous they aren't going to the FBI."

"Thank you, and I'm honored to be riding with Diego tonight. You guys all rock."

The officers broke up and headed to their cars. Officer Ramirez said, "Don't listen to those guys. That was tough and at any moment, one of us could go down for good. I'm glad they had my back."

"So am I, Diego. I wanted to jump in there myself."

Officer Ramirez laughed. "And do what? I hear you're an athlete or something, but come on. That guy was huge."

"I'm an All-Conference basketball player. I also do the 100 and 200 meters in track, but most of all, I'm a black belt, so don't get it twisted. I can hold my own."

Officer Ramirez nodded his head, "So I see. I guess there's more to you than meets the eye."

"There sure is. When I hit the academy, I won't be a pushover. I can fight. If necessary, I can run too."

"How fast? Some of these perps can run really fast."

She giggled, "My best time was 10.89 in the 100 meters."

"Wow, that's pretty fast."

"Yeah, I average around 11.1, but that 10.89 was my best. I'm more of a basketball player. I can take you to the hoop with ease."

Officer Ramirez laughed then asked, "Tell me about one of your toughest fights."

"Really?"

"Yeah, I want to see how tough you really are."

Twanda laughed, "I'm very tough."

Officer Ramirez continued, "Let me tell you mine. I responded to a meth lab. One guy was so high on PCP that anything we did to him didn't hurt him. I fought him, hit him with everything I had, even a taser but nothing put him down. I finally had to hit him with a crowbar a few times to take him down. That was the toughest fight I ever had."

"Wow, dudes hyped up on PCP are crazy. I saw one in the projects where I grew up and it was wild. There were at least ten cops trying to bring him down."

"Yeah, those are the worst kind. I was a rookie during my fight. Now, how about you?"

"Well, I was in high school. Many of the girls in the school didn't like me. I was a 4.0 student then, but most of them didn't know about my martial arts background. One week, they were harassing me on the bus. Each day was worse than the day before. So that Friday, this big girl started in and talked a lot of trash. I'll never forget her name was Harriet. So Harriet told me she was going to whip my behind when we got off the bus. I was tired of all the harassment."

Twanda giggled. "When the bus stopped, Harriet and her crew got off the bus and yelled at me. They waited for me to get off the bus. The bus driver told them to move on but they didn't. I told the bus driver not to worry, it will be over quick."

Officer Ramirez said, "Oh, you super tough."

Twanda laughed, "I'd had enough. I took one step down and dove right into Harriet's big behind stomach. I knocked her to the ground and got up. She got up, and I did a roundhouse kick to her jaw and she fell backwards. It sounded like a building toppled down. Everyone looked at me with amazement. I shouted, 'Don't ever mess with me again!' After that day, no one bothered me. Even the boys respected me."

"Yeah, that's my girl!" Officer Ramirez high fived Twanda. She smiled and laughed. No one else knew that story about her because she did not want to be judged by her past or her fighting skills. She wanted to be judged by her intelligence.

The radio blared out, "Officer needs assistance with a 502 pull over in the area of Bradford and Central."

Officer Ramirez responded, "Charlie 23, responding with assistance." He looked at Twanda and asked, "Well?"

"Drunk driving, my friend. I know all my call signs."

Officer Ramirez laughed, "I see you do. These can be interesting."

"I'll bet. Drunk people can be funny sometimes."

Officer Ramirez pulled behind the stopped cruiser. He said, "Come on, this will be fun. Just stay in the shadows and observe."

"Got you, boss." They both laughed and Officer Ramirez joined the other officer on the stop. The officer was explaining the rules to the man who was stopped.

When she finished, she pointed at Twanda and said to the man, "This is Twanda Cousins, a ride long, and she's here as an observer only. This is Officer Ramirez, and he's here to assist me with your test. Do you understand?"

"Yeah… I'm not drunk."

Twanda snickered. Her cell rang. It was a message from Melvin. The text had a video clip in it. She stepped away from the stop and watched the video. Twanda was furious. She could not believe what she was watching. Twanda closed her phone and continued to watch the test be administered to the man. She admired Officer Blaylock. She was a woman, but she showed total control and professionalism throughout the stop. *That's how I want to be. Forceful, yet professional. I want to get the job done, but I want them to know that because being a woman will not give them an advantage over me.*

After the stop, Officer Blaylock and Officer Ramirez placed the man in the back of Officer Blaylock's vehicle. Officer Blaylock asked, "How does the real thing compare to the books?"

Twanda answered, "The real thing is more informative for sure. I love the way you conducted the test. I learned more in this one stop than I did during my entire four years in college."

Officer Blaylock chuckled, "Honey, there's a whole lot more for you to learn out here. The night is just beginning."

Twanda pumped her fist, "I'm ready for it."

"Okay, you guys have a good night." Officer Blaylock got into her vehicle and drove off. Officer Ramirez and Twanda returned to their vehicle and drove away.

Officer Ramirez asked, "You want some coffee? There's an all night spot that serves a good cup."

"Sounds great."

Officer Ramirez said, "Cool. It will be good to get a cup before we head into Southeast."

"Oh, boy. I'm sure there will be some crime going on there."

"You got that right."

"I should tell you, I saw Blade earlier tonight. He was jacking up a dealer on the street. That man scares me."

"He scares a lot of people. We've been trying to put him away for a long time, but no one will testify against him."

Twanda sighed, "I heard. He's going to be a difficult case for some attorney to prosecute."

"They have tried and failed already. Here we are, Beryl's Diner. She makes the best coffee for us late night officers. She also makes a great apple pie if you want a slice."

"Oh, I love pie. Especially apple."

"Great, I'll treat."

"Thank you, Diego."

"Well, you're the ride along, so it's my pleasure. I don't know how the FBI will do it, but rookies always end up paying for the first year. I almost went broke paying."

Twanda smiled. She was enjoying her ride along. She could not stop thinking about the video and wondering how Sybil was doing. When she got a minute, she would deal with both aspects of her life.

The two sat down in a booth. Twanda asked, "We have time to eat?"

"We are on our own schedule. As long as we don't get any priority calls, we can eat. What are you having?"

"The coffee and pie are fine. I need to wash up a bit."

"Go ahead. Any cream or sugar?"

"Both thank you." Twanda went to the ladies room and called Sybil. "Hey Sybil, is everything okay?"

"Yeah, my family never sleeps, so we're all up talking about the old days. How's your ride along going?"

"Great, I'm learning a lot and having so much fun."

"Which officer did you get?"

"I got Officer Diego Ramirez."

"Oh, yeah. He's a straight shooter. I had Benson. He was cool, but something was off about him."

"I meet him but it was only for a minute or so. Well, I need to deal with something with Kenyon. I just wanted to check in with you. Get some sleep."

"Oh, I doubt that girl, but thanks. Have fun."

"Thanks, Sybil." She hung up the phone and tried to call Kenyon, but there was no answer. "*It figures. He's probably avoiding my call.*" She washed up and headed back to the table with Officer Ramirez.

Twanda sat down at the table. Officer Ramirez asked, "Is everything okay?"

Twanda answered, "Yes, why you ask?"

"In this job, you learn to read people. I can tell something is bothering you."

"It's my fiancée. My friend sent me a video of him high fiving his friends as he was telling them he had sex with me. I don't like liars."

"I get it. He's embarrassed because he feels to be a man, he has to have sex with his woman. That's so sadly wrong. I will teach my sons that being a man is taking care of your family. Sex doesn't make you a man; handling your responsibilities makes you a man."

"You're a good man, Diego. Your kids should be proud to have you as a dad."

"Yeah, well, their mom is pretty cool, too. I hope you can meet her one day."

Twanda smiled, "I hope so too, Diego. I also like how you gave her props just now. You told me it's not all you; it's your wife too. Now that's a man." Officer Ramirez nodded and ate his apple pie. Twanda took a bite of it. "Wow, this pie is awesome! You were right on point with this."

"I told you, Beryl is the best."

They finished the coffee and apple pie, then returned to the cruiser. Officer Ramirez said, "Are you ready for this last half? After three in the morning can be difficult at times."

"What does that mean, more crime?"

"No, staying awake." Officer Ramirez laughed, "Why do you think we got this coffee?"

"Got you. I'm wide eyed and loving this. I can't wait to get to the academy."

"When do you go?"

"I'm going to be in the July class. So, right after I get married, if I get married, I'll go to the academy. My fiancée is going to Los Angeles to start his business. When I graduate from the academy, I'll apply for the Los Angeles office."

Officer Ramirez popped his lips, "Sounds like a good plan. I really hope it works out for you. Don't give him too much trouble on the celibacy thing. Men can be macho at times and admitting that he hasn't had sex with you is probably making him feel less than a man."

"Really, Diego?"

"Hey, it's him, not me."

"Yeah well, we're going to have a serious talk about this video. You can believe that. He's lying on me and I don't like it."

"Definitely have a talk with him." Officer Ramirez focused on the vehicle ahead of them. "Looks like we might have another drunk driver."

Twanda looked at the vehicle, "Oh, no. That looks like the SUV I saw Blade in earlier. We might want to pass on that."

"You know how many black SUVs are in East City alone?" He did not wait for an answer, "We can't let a drunk driver loose on the road." Officer Ramirez turned on the blue lights. "Is he going to pull over or what?" The vehicle slowly pulled over and Officer Ramirez pulled in behind him. He ran the plates on his laptop. "See the plates come back to a Marlon Williams."

Twanda felt something in her stomach. "Something isn't good about this, Diego. Please be careful."

"I'm always careful. I have a wife and two kids, remember?" He grabbed the radio, "Charlie-23 requesting backup for a possible 502. A black Mercedes Benz GLC-300, license plate W-I-L-L-1. "

The radio responded, "No vehicles are in the vicinity at the time, Charlie-23."

"Roger that."

Twanda said, "Let it go Diego, please."

"I can't do that, Twanda. Stay in the vehicle. I'll check his breath and I'll see if he's drunk or not. He may just be tired. It is after three."

His words brought some comfort to Twanda, but she learned over the years to trust her intuition. Officer Ramirez got out of the vehicle and approached the SUV. Twanda could not make out anyone inside. The windows to the SUV were tinted. She jumped at the beep on her phone. It was a text from Kenyon. She read it and smiled. *"I do love you dude, but we…"*

The shot rang out in the quiet night. Twanda looked up and Officer Ramirez was on the ground, clutching his stomach. The door to the SUV flung open and a large black man stepped out. Officer Ramirez tried to get his weapon out, but the man stepped on his arm. Officer Ramirez screamed into the night. The man raised his weapon and fired two more shots into Officer Ramirez. His body went limp.

Twanda's instincts kicked in. She could not get into the driver's seat, so pushed open the door and ran as fast as she could. The shots almost hit her twice, but she was quick. She learned from the projects not to run in a straight line. She heard Blade order his men to chase her into the night.

Chapter 3

Twanda was on the edge of East City's Southeast neighborhood. She stopped at an abandoned building to see if the men were close to her. *"I need to get out of here and call the precinct for help. Poor Diego. Oh my God."*

Twanda heard a sound. She ducked, hoping no one could see her. She peeked out, and it was a couple walking toward the building. Twanda suspected they were going to have sex. She rose to warn them, but saw one of Blades men approaching. The man shouted at the teenagers, "Hey, have you seen a girl around here? She's about five, seven, athletic and can run fast as Hell."

The boy answered, "No, I haven't seen anyone, Aaron."

Twanda realized the boy knew Blade's man so he would not be of help to her. She had to stay on the move to get away from them. Aaron said, "Tonight's not a good night to be down here, Greg. You better get Donna home, especially if Mr. Danielson finds out you had her down here."

"We're out, man." The couple rushed away from the area. Twanda watched Aaron move into the building.

"If I can subdue him and get his weapon..." Before she could continue that thought, the other man arrived on the scene. Now both men were there. She would not be able to subdue both of them at once.

She suspected Blade was behind her and now Aaron plus the other man were in front of her. She was blocked in. *"I need a way out. Hopefully, I can get past them while they're in the building. If I can get into the neighborhood, I can call and get some help."* She eased out of the bushes and tried to make her way past the building. Aaron walked out of the building and fired at her. Twanda took off running again.

Aaron was behind her, but he could not keep up. He stopped and fired again. One shot hit the corner of the building as Twanda turned. She stepped into the alley and grabbed a trash can lid. She could hear Aaron breathing. *"He's clearly out of shape."*

Aaron got to the corner and Twanda swung as hard as she could, knocking him to the ground. She grabbed the gun and tried to run, but Aaron grabbed her foot and tripped her to the ground. "Now, I'm going to teach you a lesson for making me run so hard."

Twanda turned and pointed the gun at him. He said, "You won't fire little girl." She hesitated. "See, when you take a life, it changes you. I took my first life when I was nine. I'm immune to it." He stepped towards her, trying to snatch the gun. She fired two shots into his chest. Aaron stood, mystified that he was wrong. She would shoot and she was accurate, too. He fell to the ground, dead. The other man rushed around the corner. Twanda jumped up and ran again. She heard the man shout, "You killed my brother! You're dead! You hear me? You're dead!"

Twanda was out of breath when she reached the precinct. She stood out of sight and across from them. Police were rolling out in convoys. *They must be looking for Blade.* She saw Officer Baker and shouted, "Officer Baker!"

Officer Baker looked in her direction and pulled out his gun. "It's her… freeze, put your hands in the air."

Twanda replied, "Hey, it's me, the ride along."

She heard another officer shout, "There's the girl that shot Diego."

Twanda could not believe her ears. They suspected she killed Officer Ramirez. Using the building as a shield, she sprinted away, again dodging gunfire. The sirens were closing in on her position, but she knew many of the areas in Southeast. Twanda jumped fences and ran as fast as she could.

Six streets over, a lady waved her to come into her house. Twanda trusted her gut and went inside. The lady said, "You're the girl everyone is looking for?"

Twanda looked at her, "I didn't kill that officer."

"I believe you, but the people in Southeast want blood for Aaron and they have the police on their side. If they see you, they'll kill you."

"I know."

"And me."

Out of breath, Twanda said, "I suspect that."

The lady continued, "I can let you stay here for a minute, but that's all. If they know I helped you, they will kill me."

Twanda said, "I just need to catch my breath. You can tell them I held you at gunpoint." The lady did not respond. "How did I get myself into this mess?"

"My name is Ella, and it seems we often find ourselves in situations that we don't understand. My son, Brian, found himself in one of Blade's gangs and got himself killed for it. He wanted to get out of the gang, but Blade's number one rule was that you die your way out. Now I do what I can to help those in the neighborhood who don't want to conform to Blade, but I'm afraid I'm an old woman and I can't do much."

Twanda heard shouting in the streets. Gang members were looking for her. She saw the man she only knew as Aaron's brother heading them up. He directed them in several directions and they followed his instructions. Twanda asked, "What's that guy's name?"

"That's Tony Drayton. The man you killed was his brother, Aaron. He won't quit until he kills you."

"He made that clear. What I don't understand is how the police think I killed Officer Ramirez. I was in the car the entire time."

"You don't know that Blade has the police force working for him? He probably had them blame it on you."

Twanda sighed, "This is crazy." Tony walked up to the house. "He's coming this way."

"Don't worry. I'm good at lying." The knock at the door was heavy and hard. Ella eased the door open a little. "Tony, what's all this fuss about at this hour? I'm trying to sleep and I have to work in a few hours."

"We looking for a woman. She's about five seven and slim. Have you seen her?"

"Are you serious? I'm sleeping. You know I don't get involved in any mess at night."

"If you see her, you better tell me, Miss Ella."

"Watch how you talk to me, boy. I remember when you were born."

"That was a long time ago, Miss Ella, but I respect you."

"I will let you know if I see anything."

"You're looking good in that robe. If I wasn't busy, I'd come in there and check you out."

"I'm twice your age, boy; not to mention I'd rather die."

"Keep it up and you just might."

Ella closed the door and walked back into the living room, where Twanda waited. "I've bought you a few hours. You better get some rest. I believe this will be the hardest time of your life."

"Thanks, Miss Ella. I won't ever forget this."

"This in is honor of my son. Get some rest." Ella brought Twanda some blankets and a pillow. "Now this couch is very comfortable. Brian used to fall asleep on it all the time. If you need anything, I'm in the other room."

"Thank you again, Miss Ella. I appreciate." It was not long before Twanda dosed off. She slept peacefully until the loud noise in the street woke her.

She peeked out the window and there were several cars lined up. All of them were fancy cars. Blade stood in front of the group. He shouted, "Officer Ramirez was a good friend of mine. Aaron was my top lieutenant. This woman came into Southeast, our neighborhood and took two lives from us. The police want her for their man. We want her for our man. They will take her to court for something they call justice. We want our own justice; an eye for an eye." The crowd shouted their support. "Whomever brings me Twanda Cousin's corpse will receive one million dollars." The crowd went to another level.

Twanda fell back on the couch. She looked up and Ella stood there. Ella said, "Everyone is going to be looking for you now. Is there anywhere you can get help?" Twanda did not have an answer. Ella continued, "It won't be long before they put two and two together and know that you came here. I can sneak you out in the trunk of my car. If you can get out of Southeast, you might have a chance."

"That works for me. Where do you work?"

"AmeriCorp in the city. I can take you that far, then you're on your own after that."

Twanda stood up, "Miss Ella, there is one thing you can do when you get to work." Ella listened without asking what, "Can you call the FBI and tell them the truth? I know Blade doesn't own them. There's an agent I've been talking to about my recruitment. Here, her name is Hillary Wells. If you can tell her what really happened, I might have a chance."

"I'll do it. Come get in the trunk." Twanda followed Ella to the garage and got inside the trunk. She prayed Blade's gang wouldn't force Ella to open the trunk of her car.

The drive out of Southeast was slow. Twanda imagined Ella having a difficult time navigating the streets. Everyone wanted the million dollars Blade offered for her dead body. Now she had no allies.

The car came to a sudden stop and Twanda feared the worse. The trunk popped opened. No one was there. Twanda eased out of the vehicle. She saw Ella in the driver's seat and hear shouts in the distance. They were coming toward her. She rushed to the driver's seat. Ella clutched her heart. Blood oozed through her fingers. The bullet struck her. Instinctively, she must have popped the trunk so Twanda could escape.

Twanda closed her eyes and kissed her forehead. *"She was a good person who only tried to help me."* Twanda rushed to a set of nearby buildings. When she reached the buildings, the group arrived at the car. She could see them from her advantage point. They were not gang members or police. *"People trying to get rich and not caring if the person they're hunting is innocent. I've got to get to the FBI."*

"Hands up!" The voice behind Twanda felt fear in her heart. Someone got the drop on her. "Drop that gun and turn around slowly." Twanda did as instructed. "Well, well… looks like I'm about to be a million dollars richer. This way, lady." Twanda walked in the direction the man had pointed.

He ushered her into a doorway that lead to a lobby, then into an old office room. "That's far enough. Take a seat in that chair." Again, Twanda followed his orders.

"I thought the instructions were to bring my corpse to Blade."

"Yeah well, there's too many people out hunting you right now, so we're going to lie low for a minute until some of them disperse. They'll give up, then I'll take you to Blade myself and collect my million."

"How can you be sure he'll give you the million? You know his reputation. He'll probably tell everyone he killed me while they will never find your body."

"There's that chance I'll take but, I have a plan for that too. Meanwhile, baby, just chill." He pulled out some rope and tied Twanda to the chair. He cut the television on. "Now let's watch some news and see what they're saying about your pretty little self." He rubbed her on the chin and she snatched her head away.

The news reporter said, *"The suspect in the killing of Officer Diego Ramirez and Aaron Drayton is ECU's criminal justice administration major, Twanda Cousins. Twanda is an All-Conference basketball player and a member of ECU's track team. She holds a black beat in martial arts and is considered armed and dangerous. No reason for the murder of Officer Ramirez has been given. Twanda was on a ride along in Officer Ramirez's vehicle last night. After gunning down Officer Ramirez, Twanda ran off into the night where she was confronted by Aaron Drayton. Aaron tried to bring Twanda in but was fatality shot by Twanda."*

"Blade Samuels, owner of the renowned Oasis club in Southeast, has put an award of one million dollars for the capture of Twanda Cousins. Police consider this a high profile case since one of their own was murdered."

The man said, "Wow, you've been a busy young lady tonight."

"You can't believe I actually did all that. What reason do I have to kill the man who allowed me to ride in his vehicle to see the police in action? Ask yourself what's more believable in this scenario."

The man breathed a deep sigh, "You're probably innocent, but for me that doesn't pay well. The million could go a long way to getting me the life I want."

Twanda nodded her head. She used her brain power to figure a way out of the building. This man certainly only cared about the money.

The man's phone rang, and he answered it, "Ray." She presumed the voice on the other end answered. Ray continued, "Well baby, all our problems are over. I got us a gold mine. I'm just waiting for all the crazies out there to go home, then I will deliver this little honey to Blade myself." He paused, listening to the response. "That's right. I got Twanda Cousins and I'm going to kill her and take her to Blade." He paused again. "Okay, wait at home and I'll take care of the business at hand. Then we'll go somewhere and enjoy all the money we'll have to spend." He hung up the phone with a smile on his face, bigger than the state of Maryland.

"Girlfriend I take it."

"That's right, and we're going to head to Jamaica when I get paid."

"Good for you. You'll be rich at the expense of an innocent life. Your parents must be proud."

"My parents, if you must know, abandoned me when I was a child. First daddy left when I was born, then mommy left before I turned four. Neither of them cared about me. Now, I'm getting what's rightfully mine, and I don't care if you're innocent. All I care about is the money."

"That's obvious. I'm sorry about your parents. No child deserves that."

"Well, if I were you, I wouldn't waste my last hours feeling sorry for me. I don't feel sorry for you at all."

While he was talking, Twanda use the distraction to work her hands free. She was happy he did not appear to have a clue how to tie a good knot. In the outer office, she heard a noise. Twanda asked, "How much in love is that girl with you?" Ray looked at her, puzzled. "Sounds to me like someone found us. That could only happen through your so called girlfriend."

The puzzled look turned into fear. Ray eased up and looked out the window. Twanda used that moment to free herself. She grabbed her gun off the desk and pointed it at Ray, but a man and woman rushed into the room.

Twanda fired a shot, turned and dove out the window. She struck the ground hard, rolled over, and ran as fast as she could. She heard gunshots and shouting behind her, but nothing fired in her direction. *This time I'll double back. It's time I leave some bodies behind. Maybe people will think twice about hunting me.*

Twanda doubled back. Ray's body laid on the ground. A woman and a man stood next to it. The man was shot in the arm. Ray must have got him before they shot him. She heard the woman say, "Are you okay?"

"Yeah, where did she go?"

"I don't know, but we let a million dollars get away because of that fat bastard. I stayed with him all these years and for nothing."

The man said, "Don't worry, she can't be far."

She ordered, "Come on, let's go this way."

"Why that way?"

"Look on the ground. There's some blood."

Twanda eased behind them. "Drop your guns." Neither of them dropped their guns. She cocked her gun, "I said, drop your guns now!" Both dropped their guns. "So you want to get rich off an innocent person? I should kill you both here."

The woman replied, "Go ahead, because if I get the chance, I'm going to kill you."

Twanda giggled, "Ray loved you. I don't know why."

"Ray was a fat idiot. I'm sure you learned that in the time you spent with him."

"Yeah, whatever. How about you march back to the building?" Twanda herded them both back to the building, where she tied them up. "I didn't know much about Ray, but I learned he sucked at tying a knot. I don't. You won't get of that knot." She snapped the knot tight. "Good luck. Since you wanted me dead, I hope someone finds you before you starve to death." She gagged both of them and headed out of the building.

Twanda checked her surroundings. She had to be sure no one else heard the shots and dropped in on the party. As morning rose, more and more shots could be heard in Southeast. Everyone was looking to kill her and in the process, they were killing each other. *"That's probably what Blade wanted."*

She found a house that appeared to be empty. Twanda broke the lock on the back door and went inside. There was no alarm, but she figured as much since the house was in Southeast. *"Looks like no one has been here for a while. Maybe they're on vacation. Good, I can lie low for a minute."* She opened the refrigerator. There was not much to eat, but she found some deli meat and made a sandwich.

She flopped down on the couch and looked at her shin. There was a bruise on her leg from jumping out the window. She walked back to the refrigerator and grabbed some ice to put on it. Twanda cut on the television and the news reports were about her. *"My picture is plastered on every network. There's nowhere I can go.*

I'll lay low here until night. Maybe then I can get to the FBI headquarters building. Oh, what am I thinking? There has to be a computer here somewhere."

She looked around the home and found the connection where the laptop would be connected. *"They must have taken it with them. I need a phone or a computer. I couldn't have broken into a house with a computer."* She returned to the couch to sort out a plan. Before long, she drifted off to sleep.

When Twanda woke up, it was dark twilight outside. She stood and went to the bathroom to wash her face. She looked in the mirror. The scratches from the window. *"I hope I don't have any scars from this. I guess that is, if I live through it."*

She walked out of the bathroom and stopped in her tracks. The kid shouted, "Dad! There's someone in here!"

Twanda ran to the front of the house. A man stood poised with a baseball bat, looking at Twanda. She noticed the fear in his eyes. Twanda raised her hands. She placed the gun in her waist. "I'm not here to hurt you. I just wanted somewhere to lay low until I can make my way to FBI headquarters."

The man said, "You're the woman everyone is looking for?"

"I am, but I didn't kill that cop. Blade killed him and pinned it on me. I'm innocent."

A woman walked from the kitchen, "Honey, they're offering a million for her dead."

The man replied, "We're not killers, Ann."

Ann responded, "We don't have to kill her. We can call the helpline number and report her. We'll get something to help us get out of this ghetto."

"Honey, I can't sell my soul to get out the ghetto."

Ann said, "Maybe you can't, but I can." She pulled out her cell and started to dial.

Twanda whipped out her gun. "Put the phone down. Put it down now!" Ann put the phone down. "Kick it over to me." Ann complied. "Move over to your husband. Now, husband and son, toss me your cell phones." Both complied. "Now look, I don't want any trouble. I just need to get to the FBI. I know they will clear my name. All of you, take a seat."

Twanda opened one of the cell phones. "Husband, what's your name?"

"Kevin."

"Kevin, what's your unlock code?"

"0326."

Twanda unlocked the phone and dialed the number. The voice answered, "FBI, Agent Wells. May I help you?"

"Agent Wells, this is Twanda Cousins. I need your help."

"I bet you do. What the heck have you done? Everyone is looking for you."

"I didn't kill Officer Ramirez. I killed Aaron in self defense. Blade killed Officer Ramirez."

"That's not what they're saying, Twanda. They say they have evidence against you."

"There's no evidence against me. They want me dead, so I don't testify against Blade. Come get me. I'll turn myself in to you if you promise not to turn me over to the MPD."

"I can't."

"Why not?"

"Blade has more power than you know. If you can make it here, I may be able to help you."

"Are you telling me he owns people in the FBI, too?"

"I'm afraid he owns the right people. We have been given a directive not to intervene in the case. I don't know who to trust. If I make a move to you, they will kill us both. I'm sorry, but you're on your own to get here." Twanda sighed. Agent Wells continued, "Who's phone is this?"

"Some couple's house I broke into to lay low. They came home and caught me."

"You just got them killed."

"What?"

"Get out of there now. I'm sure they have my phone tapped by now and are tracing your call."

Twanda hung up. She shouted, "I held you at gunpoint and ran out of the house, which is true. If you have somewhere to go, I would go now!" She ran out of the house as a black SUV approached the house.

Twanda darted down the sidewalk as more bullets tried to find her. Her body was weary, but she had to escape to clear her name. She ran down a long alley, but a car cutoff her exit. She looked behind her and the SUV blocked the other entrance.

Twanda climbed the fence into a backyard and headed to the front of the house. The two vehicles met her there and fired on her. She returned fire. Sirens bellowed in the background. "Thank God." The police would be preferable over Blade's people. When the sirens got closer, the vehicles left.

A man stood on the porch of the house nearest to her. He said, "Hey, I can get you out of here."

"Why should I trust you?"

"You have another option?"

Twanda thought about it. If he were going to take her to Blade, he would have attacked her from behind. "Okay, how can you get me out?"

The man ran into the garage. He returned on a motorcycle. He tossed her a helmet, "Let's go."

Twanda hopped on the bike and they sped away from the arriving police cars. Twanda asked, "Can you get me to the FBI?"

"Sure, but it won't be easy. You don't remember me, do you?"

"No, should I?"

"Yeah, I was in your Juvenile Delinquency class two years ago. That's when I was trying to major in criminal justice. I switched majors after that class. My name is Toby."

"Sorry I don't remember you."

"It's okay. Blade's men are at every entrance and exit into Southeast. We'll need a plan to get out of here and to the FBI. I have a place where we can wait."

"Okay."

Chapter 4

Blade sat in his office building. It looked over the entire section of Southeast. He starred out the large window in his office with his fingers together. Blade often sat like this when he was deep in thought.

Tony walked in, "Boss, I tracked Agent Wells' number to a house on Lawnmower Drive. I sent some boys over and they said Twanda held the family at gunpoint and took their phones. She left the house minutes before we got there. We then tracked her to Sunrise Street, but the cops showed up. We think she left on a motorcycle owned by the nerdy kid everyone makes fun of on Temple Street."

"So you don't know where she is now?"

"No, we don't."

"I want you to head over to the old folks' home on Brinson. There's a Wilson Cousins living there. I want you to take a picture of him then get some posters made up. We want her to see a picture of him everywhere, so she knows we got eyes on her dad. Put on the flyer that if she turns herself in to the police, everything will be okay."

"Will do, but why the police? Shouldn't we say turn herself in to us?"

"If we say us, then people could pin her death on us. This way she'll die in police protection."

"Good idea. I'm on it."

Tony left the room, leaving Blade alone again. He walked out of the office and headed to the conference room. In the conference room were two members of the MPD and one member of the FBI. "Gentlemen and lady, we cannot have Twanda Cousins running around free. My men are looking everywhere for her, but I don't feel we're getting the support from your organizations. Pete, the FBI got a call from her, but we don't get support from you."

"Blade, we have people in place to find her. The agent she called is not one of ours, and she never would be. We are keeping tabs on her in case she tries to meet Twanda."

Officer Blaylock spoke, "We're searching everywhere for her in Southeast. All the streets in and out of Southeast are on lock down. She can't get out of Southeast without coming through our officers."

Blade was upset, "We would not be in this situation if Officer Blake would have been where he was supposed to be last night."

Officer Blaylock replied, "I have had a conversation with him. This will not happen again."

"What was he doing?" Officer Blaylock hesitated. "I asked you a question, officer."

"He was having sex with a prostitute."

Blade poured himself a drink. "So you're telling me he wasn't at the drop because he was getting some tail?" Officer Blaylock did not respond. "I don't want him talked to; I want him dead. Is that clear, Officer Blaylock?"

"Yes, sir… but killing another officer would cause an outrage."

"Then make it look like Twanda killed him. That will incite more people to find her and hopefully kill her."

"I will handle it."

Blade sighed, "Meanwhile, find Twanda. I know your shift is over, but you can't rest until she's caught; none of us can."

"I got it, Blade. I know how to conduct a search."

Blade frowned at her, "My men are posting pictures everywhere of her father. That will draw her out. I want her dead before the night is over."

"She will be, sir."

The three of them left. Blade paced the floor of the conference room, then he called Maranda into the room. Maranda was a smart businesswoman and a brilliant attorney. She strolled into the conference room. "What can I do for you, Blade?"

"We could have a problem with one of the officers. He wasn't at the drop because he was getting laid. We can't have people like that working for us. I'm having that cleaned up, and the blame placed on Twanda Cousins. Meanwhile, we need evidence that Officer Ramirez was dirty. We need something to taint his name in case we have to cover our tracks."

"I'll get on it, but it's going to be tough. He was as straight an arrow as they come."

"I know you can do it."

"I'll have Grady create offshore accounts in his name. We'll show a history of deposits going back a couple of years. We'll also throw in some off the book business to show he laundered money. I don't know how long these fake accounts will hold up, but it should last long enough for the heat to blow over."

"Good, I have faith in you, Maranda. Just get it done and brief me on what to say to the police if necessary." Maranda walked out of the room. Blade watched every step. It reminded him of his mother. She was a tough woman but held her lady like qualities better than anyone he knew.

Blade remembered his first work in his mother's organization. She sent him on a run when he was only 14. He had to take the drugs by bicycle to one of East City's meanest dealers. His mother told him, *"In order to be the man to run this organization, you need to be tough. Take this order to Brinson and bring the money back to me. If he tries anything, kill him."*

At 14, the gun looked big to Blade. He did not know if he could kill a man or not, but if he did not return having followed his mother's instructions, he would be beaten himself, maybe worse.

When he arrived at Brinson's spot, the stare down lasted hours to Blade. He remembered being scared and excited. He handed the drugs to Brinson and Brinson asked, *"What you waiting around for?"*

Blade answered, *"My money, punk!"*

Brinson and his men laughed, *"Your momma must think I'm a punk too, sending you on this run. Get out of my face."*

Blade pulled out the gun his mother gave and fired. It clicked. No bullets came out. Brinson laughed, snatched the gun, and started wailing on Blade. Blade was able to get him off, but Brinson attacked again. This time, Blade pulled his hunting knife from his boot and thrust it into Brinson's stomach.

Blood gusted out of Brinson's mouth and the others watched in amazement as this 14 year old child took down a man. Brinson's body fell to the ground. Blade looked at Brinson's lieutenant and said, *"Where's my money?"* The lieutenant handed him the money, and he returned to his mother. From that day, she called him Blade.

The phone ringing interrupted Blade's walk down memory lane. He answered, "Who is this?"

"Tony, we got the flyers and posted them throughout Southeast. I also think we got a line on where Twanda and Toby may be hanging out. He's been spotted in the old warehouses on West street. Remember where we took down Eddie and his crew?"

"I remember. Send someone over there to check it out."

"Will do, boss."

Blade hung up the phone. Tony annoyed him. Aaron was his right hand, but since his death, Tony had to take over. He thought, *"When this is all over, I will have to replace him with someone that has a backbone."*

Blade called his driver, "Bring my car around. I'm going to the Oasis."

"Yes, sir."

It was time to wind down a bit. He had everyone out looking for Twanda. Of all the things he did in his life, he could not go down for murdering a police officer. She had to die and her testimony with her.

Before going to the club, Blade changed his plans and headed to the assisted living home where his mother and Wilson Cousins lived. He arrived in his mother's room while she watched television. Her eyes widened when her big, handsome son strolled in. For one of the few occasions in his life, he smiled. "How's my favorite girl doing?"

"I'm doing good, Blade. I hear you're having some trouble."

"I am, but you know I will get control of it."

"Don't let that heifer bring you down, son."

"I won't, momma."

"You have been slacking lately, son. What is it? I didn't train you to be soft. You can't be soft in this business."

"I'm not soft, momma."

"Did you kill that officer?"

"Yes."

"You lost control. You never lose control. What's going on in your life? You can tell me."

"She's pregnant and took my child. I don't know where she is."

"Diane is pregnant?"

"Yes. I have people searching for her, but you know she's a computer geek, so she's covering her tracks good."

"You've been dating that girl now for seven years and now she gets pregnant. Why now?"

"I wanted to get her pregnant. I wanted a son to carry on the business."

"I don't understand. Why did she agree to that but leave?"

"She didn't know. I had her doctor give her birth control pills that were a placebo. She thought she was protecting herself, but she wasn't."

Blade's mom nodded her head, "That's terrible, Blade."

"She refused to stop taking the pills, so I did what I needed to do to have a son. Now she's escaped."

"Find her and get my grandchild back. Kill her if you like, but I want my grandchild."

"Yes, ma'am. I'm headed to the club to handle some business."

"Oh, I miss that place so much."

Blade smiled. "Bye, momma."

Blade arrived at the club. Since it was morning, there were few people around. The club doubled as a restaurant, and breakfast was being served. Blade spotted someone in his booth. He looked at the hostess and she replied, "He said he had a meeting with you and wanted to wait in your booth." Without saying a word, Blade struck fear in the woman. She continued, "I'll have him removed."

Blade stopped her, "Don't. I'll handle it." Blade walked over to his booth and rolled his eyes at the man. The manager arrived. He was a long-time friend of Blade. Blade said, "Cedric, there's a man in my booth. I'm about to throw him out of my club."

The man said, "I don't think you want to do that, my friend."

"Tell me, why not?"

"He has a proposition for you. You might want to listen to this one."

Blade did not know what to make of the man, so he thought he would listen. He looked at Cedric, "Fire that hostess now."

"Yes, sir."

Blade sat in his booth, never taking his eyes off the man. "What is it you propose?"

"My name is Jefferson John. My mom thought it would be funny to give me two surnames as my name. I don't think it's that funny." Blade did not crack a smile. "Anyway, you have a problem with a young lady who saw too much. I happen to know she's engaged to one of your business connections. The young man who's starting a food truck line in Los Angeles."

"How do you know about that deal?"

"Oh, we know lots of things at the FBI, my friend."

"I have an FBI agent in my organization and he was not informed of that deal."

"Come on, my friend, do you think Pete is the best we got? We have enough information on him to lock him up for years. We just haven't moved on him because we want a deal with you."

"Is that right?"

"Yes, for 30 percent of your LA business, we'll turn over the young man to you, and you can use him as bait to draw Twanda Cousins out of hiding."

"I already have bait."

"The father... yeah, that will not work out for you. He doesn't have long to live. The doctors say he may not make it through the day. You need someone who will be alive for quite some time."

Blade considered Jefferson's words carefully. He said, "I'll give you 25 percent. Bring me the man and Pete."

"Why Pete?"

"He's a liability. That's my deal."

"Okay, but Pete can't trace back to us."

"He won't. He'll be another victim of Twanda Cousins."

"Perfect. You'll have them both in a few hours."

Blade nodded, and Jefferson left the booth. In seconds, two of Blade's best women joined him at the table. Melody seductively placed her hands on Blade's shoulders and started massaging him. She said, "Honey, you're so tense. Let me work that out for you."

Blade said, "You're still working?"

"We got word that you were on the way, so we came in to be with you."

He grinned. Her hands were soft and caressing. They relaxed him. Blade eased back in the booth and enjoyed his massage and coffee. He thought about how he would kill Pete and Twanda. He needed to end this situation before it got too far out of hand.

Chapter 5

Twanda and Toby arrived at the vacant warehouse. Twanda scanned the warehouse and frowned. She asked, "Why do you hang out here?"

"During my freshman year, I got heavily into computers. I loved the action. That's why I changed majors. I needed a spot to house my equipment and stay off the grid. The FBI will hunt down a hacker like me."

"A hacker?"

"Yeah, I'm good, but there are some great hackers out there. One day, I'm going to be the best."

"Okay." She was not impressed. Hackers were criminals in her mind, but she realized his skills could come in handy at some point, so she tolerated it.

"Look, I can hack into the police files and see exactly what they have on the officer's murder. You may be able to use that information to clear your name."

"Why would you do this for me?"

"Because I always liked you. You're a great person."

"Look, I'm engaged…"

"No, no… not like that. I'm also a freedom fighter. I don't like bullies like Blade pushing people around. You want to know a secret?"

"What?"

"I know where his girlfriend, Diane, is hiding out. She's pregnant from him and he wants her back badly."

Twanda replied, "Thanks for that information, but it has nothing to do with me. I need information to clear my name."

"I'm on it. The police just upgraded their firewalls so it may take me a bit to get in. You can have a seat on that couch. It's clean."

Twanda was hesitant. She spotted a towel that appeared to be cleaner than the couch. She placed it on the couch and sat on top of it. "Toby, I truly appreciate what you're doing for me. I guess a million dollars isn't important to everyone."

"No, it isn't. That money is blood money and I wouldn't dare take it. Blade bought off the police, FBI and politicians with that money, so I won't be another one he buys off. The police have these body cams. They have to upload the footage to their computers at the end of the shift. If I can get that file, you will be cleared."

Twanda replied, "Dang it."

"What?"

"He wasn't wearing it. I remember thinking about that earlier in the night, but there were some incidents that we had to respond to, so I never got the opportunity to ask him."

"I'm sure someone filed a report on it. There has to be a record somewhere that says the truth."

"Of course, Blade wouldn't want the truth to come out."

"You got that right, but it's not all up to him."

Twanda continued to sit on the couch. The old abandoned warehouse reminded her of her days in the projects. The projects she lived in were old, but they were the best of times for her. Everyone on her block was friendly. All the mothers were her mother, too. She remembered not getting away with anything because so many eyes were on her. Now, with her virginity in tack, she was glad they were strict with her.

She dozed off when Toby shouted, "Eureka!"

"What the heck? Did you find something?"

"I did. Remember when you said the officer didn't wear his body cam?"

"Diego, yes, he didn't have it on."

"Well, Officer Blaylock did, and listen to what I found." Toby played the file back.

Officer Blaylock said, "What happened here, Blade?"

"Officer Blake didn't show up. Instead, this idiot pulled me over. He saw the bags of crack and tried to arrest me."

"You shot him?"

"I didn't have a choice."

"This is bad, Blade, this is really bad."

"Not so much. There was a girl in the car with him. My men are chasing after her… hey you got that camera on? What the Hell are you trying to do?"

"I'm…"

Toby said, "That's the end of the video, but there's enough here to get both of them."

Tony said, "Too bad no one will hear it."

Twanda's heart dropped. Toby stood with his hands up. Twanda raised hers, too. Tony continued, "You have caused us so much trouble and you killed my brother. I'm going to have so much fun with you before I had you over to Blade."

Toby said, "You can't do this."

"I don't need you alive, nerd."

"Yes, you do. I have information on Diane."

Tony asked, "What?"

"If you kill me or her, I will erase all the information I found on Diane's whereabouts. Blade will be pretty pissed at you."

"Oh, so you think you have something to bargain with? I'll shoot you and have my boys go through your computer."

"Good luck with that. If your 'boys' know anything about computers, they know I can rig mine. One wrong keystroke and everything goes up in smoke."

While the two of talked, Twanda plotted her escape. Toby was safe because he had the information Blade wanted. She wasn't safe, but she needed that video to prove her innocence.

Twanda's gun sat on a table two feet from her. She did not think they noticed the gun. While Tony and Toby exchanged comments, she eased closer to the gun. She needed to make a quick move, grab the gun, and fire at Tony. If she took him out, maybe the other two would run.

She was almost there when Tony spotted her. He shouted, "Stop!"

Twanda dove for the gun. She grabbed it and shot one of the men in the head. Tony and the other man fired back at her. She wounded the man and got the drop on Tony. He threw a punch at her. She grabbed his wrist and used his weight against him to take him down. She powered two punches to his jaw, then hit him over the head with a nearby cannister. Tony was out cold. She thought about killing him but could not bring herself to kill him since he was no longer a threat.

Twanda said, "We need to get out of here."

Toby replied, "Lead the way."

"Did you download the video?"

"I backed everything up to another location." Twanda looked at him. "Yeah, I didn't mention that part to them. I got to have an ace to play. But to answer your question, yes, I have it on this drive."

Twanda grabbed the drive. "Thanks, I'm going to need this." They rode off on the motorcycle. The explosion lit up the night sky for miles. Twanda asked, "Did you do that?"

"No, they probably tried to get into my computers. I told them it was protected."

Twanda said, "We need another safe place. One they don't know about."

"I have the perfect place." He directed his motorcycle through the streets of Southeast. Toby asked, "Where did you learn to fight like that?"

"I grew up taking martial arts classes. I'm a third degree black belt."

They pulled up to a house on the North side of Southeast. Toby pulled the motorcycle into the garage and hides it. He said, "This is my grandmother's house. Most people don't know she's my grandmother because my dad left us years ago. My mom and my grandmother don't speak. Come on inside."

They walked into the house. Twanda noticed the feel of a grandmother's spirit in the house. That smell that tells you things have been in there for years. It also told you the house had that love where grandchildren could always return to and be loved.

Twanda lost her grandparents many years ago and being in the house at that moment felt good to her. It brought back the fond memories of Grand Momma Cousins. The vision of Grand Momma Cousins holding her in her arms and telling her everything would be alright the day her mom died brought a smile to her face and sadness to her heart. She missed them both.

An elderly woman emerged from the kitchen. "Well, if it ain't my nerdy grandson."

Toby replied, "Even my grandmother calls me a nerd."

Twanda said, "It's cute."

Toby hugged his grandmother. "How are you, son?"

"I'm good, grand momma. This is my friend from school. Umm…"

"Twanda."

"Okay, we're going with the real name."

Toby's grandmother said, "I know who she is. Everyone in Southeast recognizes her. Come on in, baby. Get away from that window before someone sees you." Toby's grandmother walked to the window and closed the blinds. "I hope no one saw you come here, Toby."

"They didn't. I was real careful not to be followed."

"Good."

"You shouldn't have come here. Especially with her in tow."

Twanda turned to see who was speaking. She was a beautiful dark skinned black woman with pearl white teeth. Toby said, "I needed her to be in a safe place that no one would suspect; same reason I put you here. Twanda, this is Diane, my cousin."

"Cousin? You left that little detail out."

"I did, and you can understand why. Diane, you look good. How many months are you now?"

"Seven, but I still say you shouldn't have brought her here."

Toby reiterated, "I needed to bring her here. If push comes to shove, there's enough space in the safe room for both of you. But we have a plan to end all of this."

Twanda said, "Hey turn that up, please." The volume on the television rose.

The reporter said, "Posters of this man have been plastered all over Southeast. They say they have eyes on this man we have identified as Wilson Cousins, the father of Twanda Cousins. Mel, the reward money is causing people to take drastic measures to find Twanda."

Mel answered, "You are correct Stephanie. Police Sergeant Benson stated, 'The reward has gotten out of hand and the police are asking Blade to withdraw the reward before more innocent people are hurt.' He believes the police can safely apprehend Twanda Cousins without incident if the people of Southeast would stay off the streets."

Stephanie continued, "Thank you for that report, Mel. We hope there will be no more bloodshed and Twanda Cousins can be peacefully brought to justice.

In other news." She paused, "Also, in this case, it is suspected that Officer Diego Ramirez might have been working for a criminal element. Police have uncovered documents that show he consistently made large deposits to an offshore account. It's also believed Twanda Cousins worked for Diego's drug ring and the shooting is believed to be because of a double cross by Twanda."

Twanda said, "This is crazy. We need to get that video in the hands of the right people. Now, I'm a drug dealer? God, help me here!"

"I can tap into the news feed and broadcast it to the city, but that could take days. The best way is to get in the hands of a reporter."

Twanda said, "I certainly can't do it. My face is everywhere."

Toby added, "Me either, since they blew up my site, they know me, and Diane definitely is not going to do it."

Diane said, "They don't know I'm here. I can take it."

Toby responded, "No, there's no way you're going out there, Diane. It's too dangerous."

Twanda replied, "I can't let you do that. You're pregnant."

"A reason he won't kill me. He might be angry that I disappeared with his child, but he won't kill me until I have this baby."

Twanda walked up to Diane, "That's a brave statement, but I can't let you do this for me. I love children, and I will not allow you to endanger that child's life. You don't know what Blade may do. None of us here knows what he might do in this case. We'll find another way."

Diane replied, "I'm not afraid of him."

Twanda's face stiffened, "I know what it's like to grow up without a mother. I won't let you do it. We'll find another way."

Toby's phone rang. "Hello." He paused. "Yeah, this is Toby, but don't try to trace my number. I'm too good for that." Toby hung up the phone and looked at the pic. He sighed.

Twanda asked, "What is it?" Toby showed her the pic. Twanda gasped, "I've got to get to him."

Toby said, "It's a trap."

"I know it is. Those posters weren't put there by people living in Southeast. They were put there by Blade. I have to save my father. even if it means my life."

Toby replied, "They sent an address. It says be there in one hour."

"Give it to me."

Toby's grandmother said, "I'll be praying for you, Twanda."

"Thank you, grand momma." She turned to Toby, "Do you have a phone I can use?"

"Sure, take this burner. It's good for one or two calls before they lock on to it."

"Thanks everyone. Wish me luck." Twanda turned and walked out the door. She recognized the address and knew if she sprinted, she could get there and scope out the area before they arrived. She needed an advantage.

On Twanda's jog to the address, she remembered how she started in track. Her father loved track and field and took her to any event he could. She admired Florence Griffith Joyner and watched tapes of her record setting performances in Korea during the Olympics. She wanted to be just like her, but she could not run that fast.

She arrived at the address and secured a location where she could see anyone arriving. She kept her gun in her waist. Twanda pulled out the burner cell Toby gave her. She had no family to call except her father, but she knew the assisted family home would not allow calls at this hour. Instead, she called Kenyon. After three rings, he answered.

"This is Kenyon, who's this?"

"Hey, baby."

"Twanda, where are you? Everyone is looking for you. Did you kill that officer?"

"No, you know me better than that, Kenyon. Blade killed that officer. Now he's forcing me to turn myself in to him or he's going to kill my father."

"Your dad? I guess you wouldn't have heard."

"Hear what?"

"Baby, your dad passed away about an hour ago. I only know because they had no other number to call. You left them my number as an alternate, remember?"

Twanda was stunned. The news about her dad devastated her. She was also amazed at Blade trying to trick her into turning herself in. She asked, "Did he kill him?"

"He meaning Blade? No, he didn't. Your father didn't have much time to live. The nurse said he didn't want to burden you with knowing he was in his last days. She also said he was strong considering his problems. She was surprised he lasted this long."

Twanda was silent. She did not have words for the loss of her last family member. She said, "That's it; I don't have any more family." Tears rolled down her cheeks. "I'm all alone now."

"You're not alone, Twanda. I'm always going to be here for you. Tell me what I can do to help you get out of this mess."

"There's nothing no one can do. He owns the police, politicians, the FBI; everyone."

"Everyone can't be on the take, sweetheart."

Twanda said, "There is one thing I can do."

"What's that?"

"Kill him."

"Wait, you don't mean that. There has to be another way."

"There isn't. When he shows up here, I'm going to take him out. Even if I have to die trying."

Kenyon replied, "I can't let you…"

Twanda hung up the phone. Her mind was made up, and she needed to take Blade out. She could not see another way out of her situation.

Twanda looked at her watch. She had 20 minutes before they would arrive. *Who am I kidding? How can I take out the biggest thug in East City alone? I need some help.*

She heard a sound coming from the steps. Someone was on the rooftop with her. She moved around behind a steampipe. A man with a rifle took up a position similar to where she was to scout the territory. *"I have to take him out. I hope there's no one else on the other buildings. If it's a fight they want, then it's a fight they'll get."*

The sniper got into his position and waited with his gun pointed in the direction he believed the meet will take place. She moved slowly to get close to him. His focus would be on the shot and not on her. As long as she did not make a sound, she could get to him.

Twanda was ten feet away but tripped on a pipe. The sound caused the snipper to turn in her direction. They both paused, looking for an advantage in the showdown. Twanda moved first with one of her pattern reverse kicks, knocking the gun out of his hands.

They stood poised against each other. He threw a roundhouse right, but Twanda ducked. She countered the move with a kick to the stomach. He bowed over, struggling to gain air. Twanda struck him with an uppercut then two powerful blows to his jaws. Blood spattered on Twanda and the surrounding ground.

Twanda struck him with a sidekick, knocking him to the ground. The man rolled around while Twanda stood over him. She did not notice him pull out the knife. He swung it at her, catching her on the top part of her shoulder.

Twanda grabbed her wound and scream. The cut was painful, but she had to get herself together before he struck again.

The man made his way to his feet. He wiped the blood away from his mouth and grinned. "Now, I'm going to do you in and claim that million dollars for myself. I'm going to be a rich man, thanks to you."

"Everyone seems to say that to me today, but like I told the others, that's not going to happen."

He grinned and struck again, but Twanda sidestepped the blow. She spun around and caught the man in the face with an elbow. She took his arm, slammed it against her knee, freeing the knife. "You're probably a great shot, but when it comes to hand-to-hand, you suck." She grabbed the knife, but the man grabbed her by the ankles and tripped her down. Twanda grabbed a pipe that was sitting on the ground. She swung it around and struck the man. Twanda got up and struck him several more times until he was unconscious. She did not know if he was dead or not, but she did not care.

She looked over the balcony and saw Blade's car waiting for her. *"He won't step out unless he sees me."* She left the rooftop and headed to the street. *"Even without a plan, I'll still beat half his men."*

Twanda got to the bottom of the building. She moved through the garage area and peeked out onto the street. The lone SUV sat on the road. She scanned the buildings and nearby street crossings. No one was visible. *"Maybe he thinks the one sniper was enough to take me out. Didn't happen, brother."* She stepped out from the shadows and shouted. "Get out of the car, you coward!"

Nothing happened. *"Lord, what have I done? You know Twanda, you can be too pushy at times."* She worried she had not scouted the area well enough and someone would take her head off.

The driver's car door opened, and a man dressed in all black stepped out. He wore shades in the dark, and Twanda chuckled at the look they were trying to create. The man moved to the rear passenger side door and opened it.

Blade stepped out and adjusted his clothes. Twanda thought, *"How arrogant. Even at a meeting with no one around, he wants to look good. Maybe someone will take a picture of him killing me."*

Blade asked, "You ready to die, little girl?"

"That's what your boy on the roof thought, too. By the way, he won't be joining you tonight."

Blade chuckled and took two steps ahead, "You have proven to be a tough young lady. I'm sure you would have made a great FBI agent. Too bad we won't see that day coming. Now, if you don't come to me, I'll have to give the order to kill your dad."

Twanda laughed. "As much as it pains me, I have to say it. My dad is already dead. I was tipped off about his death earlier. You don't have that leverage to use against me."

"Then why are you here?"

"To kill you."

Blade took off his coat. "Let's see you give it a try." He tossed his coat to his driver. Before they could start, sirens bellowed in the distance. Blade shouted, "I thought I told you to hold them off!"

The driver replied, "I did. I told Blaylock personally."

Twanda shouted, "Maybe next time, dude!" She ran as fast as she could away from the area. She felt Blade and his henchman would not come after her, but she needed another plan. Somehow she needed to get out of Southeast and to the FBI.

Chapter 6

Blade slammed his fist on his 18th century prized wooden desk. "How did we allow this to happen! She was right in our hands and you let the police come in. My driver gave you distinct orders not to come into the area! What happened?"

Officer Blaylock replied, "Sir, not everyone is on your team. I kept them at bay as long as I could, but someone called 911 and reported she was in the area. Twanda Cousins is the most wanted criminal in East City right now. She's accused of shooting an officer. No cop in the city is going to stay put and wait for you to do what you want."

"Who called?"

"It was anonymous. We traced the number, but it was made using the internet and routed so many times it will take our techs weeks to unravel it."

"I want a name, then I want them dead."

"I'll add that to the list."

Blade turned, "Are you being humorous, Officer Blaylock?"

"No, sir, but you have us stretched thin to cover up something you should not have done. Killing Diego was a mistake and everyone in here knows it. They're just too scared to say it."

Blade pointed at her, "Oh, and you're brave."

"I'm a trained officer of the law. No, I'm not afraid of you or anyone else."

Blade sneered, "You're on thin ice, Blaylock."

She sighed, "All I'm saying is, if you hadn't killed Diego, we wouldn't be here trying to cover it up. What we need is her fiancée. He'll be legitimate leverage to draw her out."

"He has a deal with me. I'm his biggest investor, so why can't we find him?"

"You're trying to kill his future wife. Why would he allow himself to found?" Blade rolled his eyes at her. "We will find him. He can't have many places to hide."

"Do so." Officer Blaylock left the room, leaving Blade with his top lieutenants. "After this is over, I want her to have a fatal accident. Jimmy, handle it for me."

"Yes, sir."

Blade snapped, "I pay the MPD too much money for them to fail me like this. Where are we with the latest delivery?"

Tony stood, "I've spent the last day trying to find Twanda Cousins but I've also ensured the delivery is on time. We will be at the docks at five in the morning. The Triade knows everything about Twanda Cousins. They said we need to wrap it up, so it doesn't affect our business."

Blade popped his lips, "Everyone now thinks they can give me orders. I need to send a message and kill this girl! The longer she lives, the weaker I appear to be. Tony, I want you solely on the delivery. Troy, you take point on Twanda Cousins. We need fresh eyes on her."

Tony said, "Sir, with all due respect, she killed my brother. I want her."

Blade walked towards Tony. "Are you questioning my orders?"

"No, sir. I'll handle the delivery."

Tony sat back down and Blade continued, "Now, MPD can't find that boy either. Maranda, put a team together and find him. Don't bring him through MPD. Bring him straight to me."

"Yes, sir."

"You all have your orders." All the lieutenants left the room. Blade poured himself a drink. He thought about his rise to the top of his mother's organization and how proud she was when he took over. The first threat came when one of his mother's lieutenants tried to take control from Blade.

The man was known to everyone as Butch. Butch convinced some men to join him, and they cornered Blade and his men in an alley. The two groups fought until Blade and Butch were left standing. Blade beat the man intensely until he was within an inch of his life. He then told him, *"When Satan went to war with God, he managed to convince a third of the angels to go with him. You convinced these men to go with you. Like Satan and his angels, you and your men will die."* He shot the man in the head, then killed the other men who were against him.

Officer Blaylock interrupted his thoughts. "Sir, I have Officer Blake here to talk to you."

Blade said, "Why is he here and not handled like I asked you to do?"

"You might want to hear what he has to say."

"Speak."

Officer Blake said, "Sir, I'm sorry for not being at the drop as planned. I got side-tracked."

"This is what you brought him here to say? I should kill you both where you stand."

Officer Blaylock said, "Blade, please, let him finish. Get to the point, Blake."

Officer Blake continued, "Anyway, sir, I know where Kenyon, Twanda's fiancée, is hiding. I can take your people to him and retrieve him."

Blade contemplated his response. "If you bring me this man, I will spare your life."

"Thank you, sir!"

"Blake… if you screw up again, nothing will save you. Is that clear?"

"Yes, sir. I will not screw up again. I promise."

Blade did not respond, and the two officers left the room. Blade returned home. He called his girl, LaKeisha, "Hey baby. I just wanted to make sure you were still up."

"I am and waiting for you to return."

"I'm on my way. We still haven't caught Twanda."

"I know you're stressed over this situation, but don't worry, I will take that stress for you."

"I know you will, sweetheart. I'm on my way." He hung up the phone. No one took his stress away like LaKeisha. She was the best woman he ever had. *"One day I may marry her."*

Chapter 7

Officer Blaylock sat in her cruiser with Officer Blake. Officer Blake asked, "How did we get so deep involved with this thug? Sometimes I question why I even wear this uniform."

"We got deeply involved because we wanted money. We saw all the criminals getting more money in a week than we get in a year. Now my family is at risk because I wanted more than I had. If you screw this up, Blake, we'll both be dead."

"It will work. I know he's hiding with this girl on Mediterranean Avenue. Word has it he's been cheating on Twanda Cousins since they started dating. Twanda won't give him any." Officer Blake laughed.

Officer Blaylock looked at him with piercing eyes. "There's no time for jokes, Blake. Go get the boy and bring him back here. Then we'll meet with Blade."

"Roger that." Officer Blake got out of the car and into his cruiser. She watched him drive off and made a call.

"Hello, this is Blaylock. I need to meet with you. It's about Blade and this entire circus he's running."

The voice said, "Has he lost control?"

"Yes, and he killed Diego, not Twanda Cousins. We can't have this blow up in our face because of his temper."

"I agree. Come to our meeting place and let's talk."

"Headed there now." She hung up the phone and headed to the customary meeting place. She worried that Blade's temper with killing Officer Ramirez would blow back on all of them. Officer Blaylock was good at covering her tracks, and this time she needed to make sure she had a plan that would prevent her from going down with Blade.

Her drive through East City was uneventful. She watched some drivers swerve on the road, but she did not care enough to pull them over, nor did she have the time. She thought about the day she got involved with Blade. He took control of his mother's gang and wanted control of all the gangs. After he took control, he called a meeting with Officer Blaylock, a prominent member of the MPD.

Blade said, *"Officer Blaylock, it's nice to finally meet you. You have been a thorn in my side for quite some time."*

"Not enough; you're still on the street."

"That I am, but now I can make your life a lucrative one. If we join together, you won't need to worry about your mortgage payment any longer. I know you and your husband struggle to pay it, but now that will become a thing of the past."

She remembers how her family struggled with her husband losing his job as an architect. Following that, her son got sick. He required several procedures that drained any money the family had. Officer Blaylock had high standards, but Blade's offer was too good. She figured she could do a few jobs then get out, but the feel of the money overwhelmed her and her husband.

Officer Blaylock pulled up to the quaint coffee shop no one visited. Most of the officers on the beat went to Beryl's, but the Tameka LaShay's Coffee House was reserved for those who wanted to stay away from the police. She walked inside and there was the man with the athletic build who gave off an aura that he owned whatever establishment he was in.

He always sat facing the door, not wanting anyone to get the drop on him. Officer Blaylock preferred to face the door herself, but she always gave way to him. He said, "Cassandra, it's good to see you in person."

"Clarence, it's good to see you. Although I wish it were not under these circumstances."

"I understand, but we both knew this day would come. Blade has gotten sloppy since uniting the gangs. Too much power for one man to have. It was better when there were several gangs warring over stupid stuff. How do we do this?"

Officer Blaylock sighed, "He's bent on killing this girl, Twanda Cousins, and blaming her for Diego's death. That doesn't sit right with me."

"I didn't think that it would be for you or any officer."

"Most don't know he killed Diego. They're just acting on my instructions. I have to have vengeance for Diego and Twanda Cousins isn't the one. Blade has to die."

"Trust me, Cassandra, I will get it done."

"I know you will, but I also need to you to keep that girl alive. The only way we keep the gangs at bay over killing Blade is for her story to get out. Right now, she has no help, no support from anyone. If you come in and help her without anyone knowing, then we can make this work."

"You're asking me to work on two fronts. That will not be easy."

"I know, but it's going to come together. He's got a line on Twanda's fiancée. When he offers him up to her, she'll come to his aid. That way, you'll have both of them in one place. You can take him out, save her, and we can get her story out. Not to mention, I can get out of under his thumb and live the rest of my life in peace."

"I'm on it, Cassandra."

"I owe you."

"We're cousins. You don't owe me anything. This is what family does for one another." He rose and so did she. They embraced.

She giggled, "God, dude, you are so tall. My little five six frame is nothing to you."

"Trust me, it's not easy being six five but I make due. Take care and I'll keep you informed."

"Roger that." Clarence walked out of the shop and Officer Blaylock took his seat so she could see who entered the shop.

The server joined her, "Can I get you a coffee, officer?"

"Yes, please; cream and two sugars."

"Coming right up."

The server left to get her coffee, and she looked out into the night. *"Somewhere out there are my morals. I need to find them again and make my world right. My kids are old enough to know now and they will hate the woman I have become."*

Chapter 8

Out of breath and tired, Twanda made it back to Toby's grandmother's house. The lights were out, and she did not want to disturb them, but she needed a first aid kit for her arm. She made her way to the back door and forced it open. Toby stood in front of her with a gun. "Girl, I almost blew your head off!"

"I'm sorry. I thought all of you were sleeping."

Toby put the gun away, "No, I've been waiting for a word from you. I see you got away again."

"I did, but not without an injury. Do you have a first aid kit?"

"I do. Hold on and let me get it." Toby left the room and Diane walked in.

"Did he do that to you?"

"No, one of his henchmen did it. I left him dead or unconscious."

"How did you learn to fight so well? If it were me out there, I would be dead by now."

Twanda replied, "Training. As a kid, I practiced martial arts. I got a third degree black belt in Taekwondo. I also did some judo and karate."

"I saw you play ball and run track, too. Quite the athlete. I guess Blade got more than he bargained for when he went up against you."

"That he did."

"Did you save your father?"

"I couldn't. He was already dead. Blade set a trap for me, but my fiancée gave me a heads up."

"I'm sorry for your loss."

Toby walked back in the room, "Loss?"

"My dad passed away today. I didn't get to say goodbye because I'm on the run."

Toby replied, "I'm sorry for your loss. How did he die?"

"Natural causes. Apparently, he was in worse shape than he let on. He knew I would be alone after he passed."

Toby said, "Here's the kit."

Twanda tried to bandage her arm but Diane said, "Here, let me do that for you."

"Thanks, Diane."

Diane bandaged Twanda's arm. She wondered if her family line would end with her. *"Maybe I should have had sex. I could have at least given my dad a child before he passed. Now, I could easily be it for my family. Life sucks."*

Diane said, "There, that should hold you until you get to a hospital."

"You're very optimistic."

"I am. Blade's time is running out and this killing of that police officer will catch up with him. I trust God in that."

"You're a Christian?"

"Yes, I strayed off the path while I was with Blade. The money made my life exciting, but I'm finding my way back. This baby changed everything for me. When I realized I was pregnant and who the father was, I knew I couldn't raise my child in that life. There was nothing but pain and death around us. It was fun when I was young; being able to go anywhere I wanted, buy what I wanted and had no job, but now I'm looking at my child and wondering if I have sentenced him to death before he's 21."

"I get it. Blade will certainly have him in the family business."

"More than you know. His mother trained him to run the business, so I'm sure he wants to train his son."

Twanda said, "That's sad."

Diane continued, "His father died when he was only three years old. He died on the streets trying to run a gang. That's when his mother took over. She then trained him to take over the family business. His mother put big ideas into his head, but I don't think he can live up to them."

"Well, if I can help it, he won't live at all. He killed Diego and now I've been running and fighting for my life ever since. I can't believe so many police officers are behind him."

Diane sighed, "Girl, if you only knew."

"I watched this officer work a DUI stop before Diego died. I admired her work ethic, her professionalism and everything. I thought she was awesome but come to find out she's dirty. I don't know if I want to be an FBI agent any longer."

"You're talking about Officer Cassandra Blaylock."

"I am."

"She shouldn't be working for Blade. If she knew what I know, she wouldn't be working for him."

"What do you mean?"

"I mean, Blade and his people put her in a tough financial situation. Her husband lost his job because Blade asked his boss to fire him. Add to that, they had medical bills for their son. The medical bills should have been paid by insurance, but Blade paid off some people to deny her claims. He forced her into a corner, then offered her a way out. If she knew Blade created the circumstances of her accepting to work for him, she wouldn't be working for him. She'd be trying to put him away or worse… kill him."

"Wow, what doesn't this man have his hands into."

"He's got hands on everything and everybody. Even if you get that footage to the police, it will probably disappear."

Twanda asked, "What about you?"

"What do you mean?"

"You're living evidence of his crimes. You can testify against him."

"I would be dead before I got to court. The only way to be rid of Blade is to kill him."

Twanda wondered if her words were right or not. She struggled hard to stay alive, but for what? She had nowhere to go or no one to turn to for help. Even if she made it out of Southeast, the FBI likely would get the footage and destroy it. She needed to see that it was played everywhere. She asked Toby, "Can you get back to that footage and download it?"

"I've been trying, but grandma doesn't have the state of the art computer system here. If I can get to ECU, I can use those computers to download it. Once we download it, we can upload it to the internet. Everyone will see it."

Twanda responded, "ECU is outside Southeast, but I have a plan to escape."

"What is it?"

"It's a rough run, but if you can keep up, we can get there. Can you swim?"

Toby sighed, "Yeah, but... please don't say we're going to cross the river?"

"They won't expect it."

"I know they won't. Remember this when you become that famous FBI agent."

Twanda nodded in a negative manner, "Yeah, thinking twice about that now. Maybe a lawyer, so I can prosecute people like Blade and Officer Blaylock. How about an assassin, so I get rid of them?"

Toby and Diane laughed then Toby asked, "Hey wait, you're kidding right?"

Twanda laughed and walked to the bathroom. She wondered if she was kidding. Did this nightmare situation turn her from a Saint to a sinner? She had to believe it did not.

Twanda returned to the kitchen where Diane and Toby waited. Diane wanted to go on the mission to the university, but Toby was against it. Twanda said, "There's no way we're bringing a pregnant woman on this trip. It's going to be tough enough as it is."

Toby joined in, "Exactly, and we know what will happen if Blade finds you."

Diane said, "I want to help."

Twanda replied, "Stay on the television. Give us any updates that we may need. You can call Toby's cell. They don't know his burner number."

Diane responded, "Will do. Good luck, guys."

Twanda answered, "We don't need luck; it's time to trust God."

Diane smiled, "Amen."

Toby said, "Well, I'm not one for believing in God, so let's take some insurance."

Twanda said, "Where did you get that gun?"

"I kept it in the basement for insurance."

"You could have told me that earlier. I would have love to have had it with me when I faced Blade and his men."

Toby said, "I know, but I'm still worried he might find Diane."

Twanda nodded her head, "I understand. Let's bounce."

Diane asked, "Wait, can we pray?"

Twanda nodded, "Sure."

Toby added, "I'll wait for you at the back door."

Twanda rolled her eyes, "Dude, get in here. You know you were raised in the church."

Toby begrudgingly made his way over to the ladies. Diane said, "Dear Heavenly Father, we join hands tonight to ask you for your protection of my cousin Toby and our friend Twanda as they go forth in an effort to clear my sister's name. Lord, the enemy has come against her, but you have given her strength to survive this long, and we believe you will continue to bless her. We know, Lord, that my cousin has questioned his faith, but inside he knows you. Bless him and protect him, Father. Allow him to see that you are ever present in the world. In your wonderful son Jesus' name, we all pray and say... Amen!"

Twanda and Toby said, "Amen."

Twanda hugged Diane, "Thank you for that prayer. It means a lot to know another sister is praying with me and for me."

"I messed up my life hanging with Blade. I left the house of the Lord for money and the fast life, but I will return as soon as he's gone. This will be my time to be free of him. So, thank you for standing tall against him. I believe God is with you and He will not forsake you."

Toby said, "Amen."

Twanda asked, "I thought you didn't believe anymore?"

"Hey, any advantage helps."

They all laughed. Toby said, "Now let's get out of here before the sun rises."

The ladies giggled at his impatience and Twanda said, "Yeah, let's go." Twanda and Toby headed out. Twanda's plan would be difficult for them to navigate and get to the university, but she had to get there and reacquire the footage that could clear her name.

The sun was climbing and daylight of the second day would make it harder for them to get out of Southeast. More eyes would be searching for them. She prayed Toby would not have to sacrifice his life for her to live. She would not want that. Instead, she needed this to end without further bloodshed, unless it was Blade's blood. Twanda was a true saint, but the last two nights tested her faith.

She remembered her first time coming to the altar. On that day, she gave her life to Christ. Many of the church wondered if a 12 year old could understand the gravity of her choice. Twanda not only understood it but she strived to live it all of her life. Despite watching the older members of her church carry on in ways that did not live up to God, she pressed forward with her dedication.

She recounted when she was 16. Twanda left the church after choir rehearsal but returned because she had left her phone. She wondered why the church musician and the choir director's cars were still in the parking lot but blew it off, believing they were working on music.

When Twanda walked into the sanctuary, she was stunned to see them rolling across the floor half naked. When they saw her, they quickly got up and dressed, embarrassed at their actions. Twanda was appalled. They were leaders of the church and both were married. She questioned her dedication to God, but quickly decided their actions would not be her own. Shortly afterwards both quit, the church.

Now, here she was again, wondering if her thoughts lined up with God. She wanted Blade dead, but he was a human being and she did not believe praying death on anyone was right. She thought, *"Lord, please get me out of this situation without further loss to those I love and who support me. I do not wish death on anyone, but please lead me to freedom. In Jesus' name, Amen."*

They arrived at the river without challenge. It was a 50 meter swim across. Twanda knew her athleticism would enable her to make it. She questioned Toby's ability. By the look in his eyes, Toby questioned his ability too. She said, "Toby, you can do this. It seems hard, but 50 meters is not that long."

"I hope you're right, Twanda. I'm not the athlete you are, that's for sure."

They both had dry clothes in their backpacks. Twanda put her shoes in her backpack and eased into the water. "Toby, come on, bro. We need to get across before the sun rises completely."

"Okay, I'm coming!"

Twanda watched Toby gently get into the water. She giggled, watching him. He shouted, "Not funny, Twanda."

"Come on, dude." Twanda was 20 meters into the water when she saw two men come out to the shore. She shouted, "Toby! Come on, they've spotted us!" Toby looked behind him and gained his confidence. Twanda watched the men get in the water after them.

She swam as fast as she could, hoping Toby was behind her. Twanda reached the shore and tossed her backpack ahead of her. She looked back and Toby was right behind her. "Thank God," she said. She pulled out her weapon and fired several shots into the water, hoping to slow down the men chasing them.

Toby ran ahead. Twanda nodded her head, realizing she could not count on him in a fight. She grabbed her backpack, fired two more shots for general principle and ran to catch up with Toby. Once she believed they got away from the men, she stopped. "Dude, you left me?"

"You're far more capable of holding your own than I am. I figured if I got ahead of you, I wouldn't be in the way."

"Gee thanks." She loved that Toby thought so much of her, but she thought her time might be running out. She could feel the fatigue residing throughout her body. The swim across the river would have been nothing if she were fully rested, but she was not. Instead, it moved the needle closer to empty. They had to continue on. Blade would know she escaped Southeast and expand his men to catch them.

They changed clothes, and she noticed Toby trying hard not to look in her direction. She grinned and appreciated him not trying to get a glimpse of her in her underwear. "Let's go, Toby." They started walking toward the university. She calculated it would take them an hour to get there. "Hey, thanks for not sneaking a peek back there. You're a real gentleman."

Toby smiled, "Don't think the thought didn't cross my mind, but I wouldn't want to see you that way. Now, if we were in a relationship, that would be different."

Twanda smiled, "You're cute, but I'm taken."

"Where is he?"

"I don't know. He's all I have left in this world. I just hope Blade doesn't know about him."

"Hmm, Blade seems to know everything."

Twanda popped her lips. "That seems to be true. He's paid so many people off who know what he doesn't know." They stayed off the main roads and made their way to the campus. Toby knew the computer room better than any room at ECU. They got inside with all the other students and took a seat at one of the tables. Twanda asked, "What now?"

"These are just average computers. We need something with a bit more power to do it. We're here to steal a key card from one of these geeks, then use it to get inside the main computer room."

Twanda giggled, "You're joking, right?"

Toby looked around, "No, I'm not."

She asked, "Why would they have a key card?"

"Not all of them are students. Some are PhD candidates and they need the powerful computers for their work." He rose from his seat, "Stay here, I'll be back."

Toby moved to a young lady who clearly was concentrating on her work. He eased down beside her and smiled. Twanda thought, *"Who is this guy?"* She continued to watch him make his moves and in minutes he had the young woman blushing. *"I clearly didn't know this man's talent."*

An alert went off on the computer Twanda sat at. It was a news report with a picture that made Twanda struggle for her breath. She turned up the volume, and the reporter stated people in Southeast were holding Kenyon. If she did not call the number provided, they would kill him. *"Oh, my God. This will never end."* She wanted to pop up and leave, but she had to wait to see if Toby was successful. She continued to watch him work, but she worried he would not move fast enough.

Twanda paced the floor. She pulled out the burner cell Toby gave her and dialed the number. A voice answered, "This better be you."

"Let my fiancée go."

"As soon as you arrive, so I can bury you and end this."

"I'm going to bury you. I have proof you murdered Diego and you're going to pay for it."

"Bring me that evidence and yourself, or he dies."

Twanda thought, *"If I expose him, Kenyon dies. If I go to the meet, we both likely will die. Lord, help me. What do I do?"* She continued, "I'll be there in an hour. If he's hurt, then I will release the information to the world. If not, you set him free, then you can take me."

"You think you can bargain with me?"

"How do you come out of this if I release my evidence?"

"How do I know you even have evidence?"

Twanda thought, *"Dang it, he would be a little smarter than I thought."* She continued, "Give me an hour and I'll show you my evidence."

The line went quiet for a few minutes until Blade started, "You have one hour to produce that evidence, then we'll talk."

"Deal. Oh, by the way, I'd take that million dollar reward off the table too. You wouldn't want me to die before you get the evidence, would you?"

Again, the line was quiet. She knew she had him where she wanted him. "You're right, but if there is no evidence, you both will die a tragic death."

She hung up the phone, not needing to hear anymore from him. Toby continued to laugh and talk with the young woman. *"What the heck is taking him so long?"* Finally, he got up and made his way back to Twanda. She nodded her head in disbelief, "It took you that long to get the key?"

"Oh, I had a key a while ago. I was making plans to go out with her. She's just my type." Twanda rolled her eyes at him. Toby said, "I'm sorry. How inconsiderate of me. Let's get moving."

They walked out of the lab and headed to another part of the Computer Science building. Twanda said, "Blade has Kenyon. He's going to kill him if I can't produce the evidence and myself in an hour. The upside is he's pulling the reward off the table so people won't be looking for me."

"That's the upside?"

"Hey, any victory we can get is good."

Toby stopped before entering a hallway. He said, "Okay, the computers are down this hallway, but the problem is going to be getting in and out without being seen."

"Why?"

"They don't let anyone use these computers. If we get caught, we will be in big trouble."

Twanda said, "Got it. Let's just walk down the hallway to the room we want, like we belong here. I've learned in life that if you don't act suspicious, no one will bother you."

Toby took a deep breath, "Okay, let's do it."

They headed down the hallway. There were not many doors in the hallway. The glass doors were at the end of the hallway. Twanda swallowed hard when an older man walked out the glass door. Twanda suspected he was a professor in the department. He wore a white robe and was concentrating on some papers he had in his hand. She prayed he wouldn't notice them.

Toby walked up to the door and swiped the card. The doors unlocked and they walked inside. Twanda silently said, *"Thank you, Jesus."*

Twanda admired the computers in the room. They were not what she imagined. Toby jumped behind one computer and started pecking away at the keyboard. Twanda said, "Hey, once you get the file, don't upload it until I tell you."

"What? Why?"

"Remember, they have Kenyon, and I need to show proof to Blade that I have evidence against him. Then he'll trade that evidence for Kenyon's life."

"Right, I see. You know he'll kill both of you, right?"

"I know he'll try, but I have a plan."

"What?"

"Just get me that file, then I want to get you out of this. I don't want you getting hurt."

Twanda watched Toby work his magic on the computer. She admired people who held that skill. She always wanted to learn it herself, but she never had the time.

Twanda's thoughts wondered to the day she realized she loved Kenyon. He was different from other men who she dated. In the beginning, most guys said they would be in a relationship with her without sex, but only Kenyon stayed true to his word. It bothered her he would not tell his friends the truth about their sexual relationship. To Twanda, it was great to honor God's word. To Kenyon, it was an embarrassment.

Now all she wanted was to save him from Blade, and she would give her life to do that. But hopefully it would not come to that..

Toby said, "I got it! I told you these computers were fast and powerful."

"Can you download it?"

"Yeah, I have a drive."

Toby started the download. Before long, the download reached 90 percent, but something did not feel right. The room spun. She wrapped her shirt around her nose. Twanda looked around. The others in the room fell to the desk or to the floor. The download was complete. She grabbed the thumb drive. Toby's head hit the keyboard. Twanda knew they would not hurt him. She turned and got out of the room. Two men were approaching the room. There was only one way out and they blocked the path.

She looked in the opposite direction. A window was at the end of the hallway. She ran as fast as she could and jumped shoulder first through the glass. When she hit the ground, she rolled over a few times and grabbed her shoulder.

The gunshots pounded the ground around her. She got up and ran in an erratic pattern. When she was far enough away, she stopped and dropped to one knee. Twanda grabbed her shoulder, hoping it would stop the pain. It did not.

She pulled out the burner and dialed the number, "Still alive, I see."

The sternness was clear in her voice, "You thought you could kill us and get the evidence yourself. Well, you're wrong and now you're going to pay for it."

"Pay? Remember, I have your fiancée."

"I didn't forget that fact. I'm headed to Lawrence Park. I'll be by the wading pool. You bring Kenyon and the million you put on my head. I'll bring the evidence. If I see anything out of line, this evidence goes to every news outlet in the world."

"You didn't have time to set that up."

"You'd be amazed at technology these days. Why don't you ask your tech crew?"

"I'll bring Kenyon, but I'm not giving you a million dollars."

"Bring the money and Kenyon." She hung up the phone, expecting him to adhere to her request. She made her way back to Southeast. It was relaxed now that Blade removed the bounty from her head, but she still needed to stay in the shadows. She did not want a trigger happy police officer to put a bullet in her before she could clear her name.

Once inside Southeast, she quickly arrived at Lawrence Park near the wading pool. She scouted the area to make sure she picked the best advantage point. Blade would have men placed in positions near their location to take her down. The wading pool area stood in the open. Trees were a hundred yards away in any direction. She felt safe here. She could also see Blade and Kenyon approaching the area.

Twanda waited patiently for Blade's arrival. Her burner rang, and she answered, expecting it to be him. "Hello."

"Why did you leave me?"

"You were unconscious, and I didn't think they would hurt you at this point."

"Well, they didn't. Where are you?"

"I'm at the meet."

"There's something you don't know, Twanda, and I'm not sure how to tell you."

"Make it quick."

"Well, it's about…"

"It'll have to wait, Toby. They're coming."

"Twanda…"

She hung up the phone as the two men arrived at the pool. She looked Blade up and down. He was tall and muscular. She understood why people feared him. He said, "Where's the evidence?"

"Where's the money?"

"I don't understand. From everything I have learned from you, desiring money doesn't fit you."

"The money isn't for me. It's for Diego's family. You murdered him, then you made it look like he was a bad cop."

"How do you know that?"

"There's more on this evidence than you know. It was a friendly conversation between you and Officer Blaylock."

"You have the cam footage."

"I do."

"I see." Blade motioned for the briefcase. He opened it and showed it to Twanda. "To bad you'll never see any of this money."

"I told you how this works. Me, Kenyon and the money walk away. You get your evidence."

"Yeah, see, I have men placed in every direction. I've learned how fast you are; athletic too, but this time you won't get away. Is that right, Kenyon?"

Twanda looked at Kenyon. The smiled she fell in love with was not there now. She asked, "Kenyon, what's going on?"

"He's my biggest investor, baby. I can't do my business without his backing."

"What have you done?"

"I'm sorry, baby."

Blade intervened, "Let me tell you. Kenyon here has not been held against his will. He's here voluntarily. Now you're going to give me that evidence and come with us. We can't very well kill you in the open here, but we can take you back to our place and arranged a little accident for you." Blade snickered at his words, "Now, Kenyon, get your girl and let's go."

Kenyon walked toward Twanda and took her arm. Twanda looked at him with disgust. She could not believe the man she loved turned on her. Now he helped deliver her into the hands of the worst criminal East City has ever known. Her life only had minutes remaining. She had no way out of it.

Chapter 9

Officer Cassandra Blaylock heard reports of Blade and Twanda meeting in the park. She called Clarence to her home to discuss their plan. He was late, which was something rare with him. She dialed his number again, but there was no answer. *"Something is certainly wrong. Clarence is never late to a meeting."*

Her phone rang. It was Blade. She thought about not answering, but that would not be a good move at this point. She clicked the green button and took a deep breath. "Hello."

"Cassandra, Officer Blaylock... whatever you desire to be called. Your friend won't make it to your home. I must admit, I didn't expect you to try to kill me. I'm so disappointed in you."

"What did you expect? You think I don't know that I know about your plan to kill me?"

"You're right Officer Blaylock. This is a mess for both of us, but it will all be over soon. Right now, you have some work to do at police headquarters. That body cam footage is on your server. Twanda's friend was able to hack in and download it. Fortunately, I have it and her. She will soon be dead, but we have to take care of that footage on the server first."

"I'll check it out. It will be hard to remove the footage. Once those body cams are uploaded to the server, it's next to impossible to get rid of them."

Blade chuckled, "Next to impossible means that there is a possibility. Get it done, Officer."

"I will, but remember, it's been two days. We don't know who's seen it already."

Blade sighed into the phone, "Do I need to tell you what to do about that? Anyone who's seen it can't live to testify."

Officer Blaylock became exasperated, "What are you going to do with the girl in the meantime?"

"Nothing, until I know there are no more copies of the footage. I'm having her hacker friend picked up, too. I can't kill her without knowing the truth."

"I understand. I'll call you when I have retrieved the footage and taken care of anyone who's seen it. That number could be large and we can't kill them all."

"Handle it."

Officer Blaylock hung up the phone. She sighed in disbelief. Blade had eyes everywhere, and now it cost Clarence his life. She and Clarence grew up together in East City. They were more than just cousins. Their friendship endured many turns growing up. If anyone would have her back, it would be him.

The day she met him was etched in her mind. Caroline James bullied her every day. This day was like any other. She got off the bus on her way home from school. Caroline confronted her again. Like every day before, Caroline's crew always backed her. Today this tall, light skin boy stepped up and told the crew no one would jump into the fight. If they did, they would have to go through him.

Officer Blaylock remembered how his words inspired her. She knew this would be the time for her to make her mark in the community. She fought the bigger Caroline like her life depended on it. It did, and she won. She caught Caroline with a right to the jaw, then several body shots and a powerful uppercut that put her down for good. Officer Blaylock was a hero to many. It turned out she was not the only one who Caroline bullied. From that day on, Caroline never bullied Officer Blaylock or anyone else.

After the fight, the tall light skin boy introduced himself as her cousin. She had never met him or his family before they moved to East City. Now she not only had a friend, she had more family to rely upon.

She got in her Jaguar F-Pace and headed to the precinct. Getting that footage would be impossible, but necessary. Her voice was on that footage and the incriminating conversation would send her to jail for a long time.

She pulled up to the precinct. Officers were milling around outside. She walked up and asked, "What's going on?"

"There was a body found in an abandon building in Southeast. They said its Clarence Sutton, your cousin."

Officer Blaylock dropped her head. She could not let on that she already knew he was dead. They would wonder how she knew, so she had to play it this way. She burst into tears, covering her face with her hands. Officer Blake consoled her. While he talked to her, her mind was focused on getting that body cam footage back. She had an idea, but it would take some bribery to do it.

"Thanks Al, I appreciate it." She walked inside the precinct and headed to the videographers' officer. The footage is uploaded and reviewed. If there is anything suspected, it's forwarded up the chain. Officer Blaylock hoped they had not reviewed her footage because of the search for Twanda Cousins.

She knew Ken Paul from the day he joined the police department. She hoped he would be at a place in his life where a few dollars would go a long way.

Officer Blaylock walked into the office. Ken was working alone. She said, "Hey, have you gotten to the footage from my body cam? The one from the night of the shooting." Ken hesitated to answer. Officer Blaylock continued, "Ken?"

"I got it and it scared me. You're working for Blade?"

"Look, I got in over my head. That footage will destroy me and my family. I need you to delete it."

Ken sighed, "I can't do that. I could get fired."

"They would never find out, Ken. I have money and can make it worth your while." Ken nodded his head negatively. She had to convince him, "How much would it take Ken?"

"I don't know Cassandra. I just started here. I have a wife and two kids to feed. I can't go to jail."

"Look, you tell me how to delete it, then leave the room. Later today, I'll have an envelope delivered to you. Name your amount." Ken continued to hesitate, but now she noticed he was about to take that leap. If she deleted the file, he could get away with it and get paid. She did not care if she added one more crime to her list, but she did not want Ken to go down.

He said, "Okay, I'll tell you how to do it. I didn't move the file because I didn't want you to get in trouble. That could get me fired as well." He paused.

Officer Blaylock let him gather himself. "So the files are downloaded to the server in the file room. If you go into the file room and use this, it's a demagnetizer, it will erase the drive. There are only three people with access to the drive, but if you put this demagnetizer next to the drive, it will erase all the files."

"Won't that lead to more questions? Shouldn't we only erase the one file?"

"You can't access the drive without a user's password. That's a good thing for us because we can do it now. Next month they're moving to multifactor authentication. It would be impossible to get in the file room and do this."

"Okay, so go in and put this next to the drive. It will erase everything on that drive."

"Correct. Your file is on drive Alpha, Serra, 13546."

"Thanks. How do I get in the file room?"

"That's where I accidentally leave my key card on my desk while I go to the men's room. My key card will grant you access."

Officer Blaylock popped her lips, "How much?"

"Two hundred and seventy-five thousand."

"Interesting. Why that amount?"

"What I'm doing could cost me five years of my life. I make 55 thousand a year. Over five years, that's 275 K."

"I got it. You'll receive it today."

"I hope so, Cassandra. Now, I'm headed to the men's room."

Officer Blaylock watched him leave the office. She grabbed the key card and headed to the file room. Officer Blaylock passed several officers along the way, passing along their condolences. She froze when Sergeant Benson met her. "Officer Blaylock, Cassandra… I heard you were in the building, but I don't know why."

"I came down when I heard about my cousin, Clarence. I just wanted to find out all I could."

"I understand, Cassandra. We have people on it. You know the detectives will give it top priority." He patted her on the shoulder. "I'll see you tonight."

"Yes, sir." She hated keeping her criminal life from him, but she knew it was necessary. A straight arrow like Sergeant Benson would arrest her in a minute. She arrived at the file room. Officer Blaylock looked around, hoping not to draw suspicion, when her phone rang. It startled her. She regained her confidence and answered the phone, "I'm right in the middle of something. Can it wait?"

"Just checking your progress. I'm looking at this pretty little girl who's the sole living witness against me. Shall I kill her?"

"Not yet. I'm about to erase the evidence. Did you retrieve the hacker?"

"Not yet. Apparently, anyone we try to capture these days finds a way to escape us. My men are on it, though."

Officer Blaylock sighed, "You need to get him."

"I will. Just handle your end."

"I'm in the room now. I'll talk later." She hung up the phone and searched for the drive. She found it and held the demagnetizer against it. Nothing seems to happen.

A voice from the other side of the room said, "Are you expecting to erase the evidence against you and Blade?"

Officer Blaylock let out a deep breathe. She was caught in the act and there was no way out. She slowly turned around. "Blake, what are you doing here?"

"I know as much as you do about evidence and body cams. A friend of mine warned me about several hacking attempts into our servers. The hacker had to be one of Blade's people because they were really good. I camped out here until the culprit showed themselves. I had my money on you, by the way. Only someone like you could have gotten in here to wipe the drive."

"What do you want?"

"My life, for starters. A little more money than I've been getting."

"Where is the file?"

"Oh, it's safely tucked away where no one can find it. I want some reassurance before I let anything go."

Officer Blaylock popped her lips, "Blade will not like this. He's holding Twanda Cousins right now. He's also looking for the hacker, so I'm sure he'll have him, too."

Blake smiled, "So, it wasn't Blade's people hacking the server. Hmm, interesting."

"No, it was Twanda's hacker. That evidence clears her and convicts me and Blake. I need that file, Blake."

"I realize you need it. I need more money."

"I don't have more money for you."

Blake nodded his head, "Not the answer I was looking for." He paused, "Look, Officer Hibler will be back in a minute. He'll wonder how both of us got into this very secure room. There will be a lot of questions which will point a lot of fingers. That means I'll have to turn the evidence over just to clear my name."

"I'll get you more money. Just give me the file."

Blake laughed, "I'm not a fool. I'm not handing the file over until I get paid. Let's take a ride."

"Let's." The two headed for the door. They got out and down the hall as Officer Hibler returned to his post in the file room. Officer Blaylock thanked God for escaping, but then questioned her thankfulness to Him because she was not living a righteous life.

They arrived at Officer Blaylock's Jaguar and got inside. Officer Blaylock asked, "Where to?"

"The money."

"I'll have to call Blade."

"You do that."

Officer Blaylock called from the car phone. "Blade, we have another issue."

"What do I pay you people for?"

"Blake has the file. He got it off the server before me. He'll give it to you, but he wants to be paid."

Blade screamed, "I will kill him with my bare hands!"

Blake said, "That wouldn't be wise, my friend. I have the file with a friend whose finger is on the trigger. If he doesn't hear from me in an hour, that file goes viral."

"Blaylock, bring him to me."

"We're on our way." She hung up the phone. "You know he's going to kill you, right? No one crosses Blade."

"He'll kill us both unless we work together."

Officer Blaylock saw an opening. "What do you suggest?"

"You help me get the money and get out of there safely. I'll split it with you fifty, fifty."

"How much are you asking?"

"A million. That's what he was offering for the girl, so that's what he should pay for the file."

"That's not enough."

Blake pepped up, "What? How much then?"

"Two million."

"Wow, that's very ambitious."

Officer Blaylock sighed, "Look, he wants… no needs that file. He's got the girl and almost has the hacker, but without the file nothing matters. He has two million, ask for it."

"Okay, two million then. That's one million each."

Officer Blaylock nodded her head, "We have a deal, my friend." Inside she would find a way to cross him. She needed to tie up loose ends for herself. If Blade killed the hacker and Twanda Cousins, she could get the file and kill Blake herself. She would also need to take care of the man waiting by the phone for Blake. *If I can pull this off, I will have two million dollars and no witnesses alive to testify against me. I just need a little luck from the universe.*

Chapter 10

Twanda sat alone inside a damp room. She wondered if there was mold in the room. When she was a child, she was exposed to mold over a prolonged period. It caused her to come down with asthma. The struggle to breathe was something she never forgot. *"Lord, if I live through this, please don't let me come down with breathing problems again."*

Her life continued to play out in her mind. Memories of the times she had with her father in the projects. She thought about her father and not having the opportunity to say goodbye to him. *"Now, with all of this going on, he will be buried by the city, and no one will be at his funeral."* A tear rolled down her face at the thought of her father's lonely funeral. She never gave a thought to the fact that her funeral would be lonely as well. Looking out for others over herself was always her strong suit.

Twanda heard voices in the other room. She recognized Blade's voice screaming into the phone. Whatever he planned was not going the way he wanted. That thought made her smile. *"If I'm going to go out, then I'm glad whatever he's planning isn't going in his favor."*

The dripping water in the corner of the room reminded her of her old church in the projects. She used to stare at the dripping water when the pastor was giving his long sermon. The dripping would hypnotize her, and she imagined being in faraway places, doing great things for the world. Even as a child, she wanted to be an FBI agent. Now she questioned that career path. Seeing so many corrupt cops turned her stomach. The door to the room opened and Kenyon walked inside.

"Hey, baby. Here's something for you to eat." She knocked it out of his hands and looked away from him. Kenyon continued, "You don't understand the pressure I'm under to be successful. My family told me from birth that I would be the one to make it. When I blew my knee out playing football, my only option was to start a successful business."

"You had other options."

"I didn't. Do you know any banks that, even with a solid business plan, will loan me the money? How about investors?" Twanda did not answer. She knew it would be hard to get financing for his business, but she believed he could have done it on his own. "I take it by your silence that you agree. No one would give me the money except Blade."

"There were other programs that you could have pursued. You took the easy way, but what you don't realize is you will never be successful under his thumb. He will control your business. Heck, he will probably use your trucks to distribute drugs."

"Blade and I had that discussion, and my business will be clean. He's looking to expand into clean business."

"Right."

Blade walked into the room, "Kenyon is right, I am looking to expand my business, but I lied about how I'm going to do it."

Kenyon asked, "What?"

"Shut up. I'm expanding into the California marketplace. Hiding my drugs in those trucks will give me the advantage of selling my product in the open. Police will never suspect it, especially with a reputable man like Kenyon running the operation. After he's successful in Los Angeles, we'll expand to other major California cities and start a franchise here in East City. Imagine East City will become the hub of the East coast drug traffic."

Kenyon shouted, "You promised me!"

Blade frowned, then grabbed Kenyon by the throat, "I have your plan and all that I need to start your business. What I don't need is you. One more cross word and you'll die with your girlfriend." He let go of Kenyon and Kenyon gasped for breath. Blade turned his attention back to Twanda. "You have been a thorn in my side for the past few days. I'm going to enjoy killing you."

"I hate you."

"Aww, is that anyway for a nice Christian girl like you to talk?"

"I'm a Christian, which means Christ-like. I'm sure you don't know a thing about that."

"Oh, I know more than you think. My uncle ran a church scheme for years. It's a good way to get money from suckers and fools like you. He died a rich man while people starved a few houses away. I loved it."

"You're such a jerk."

"I always told myself that if this drug thing didn't work out, I'd preach the word of God and just have people give me their money."

Twanda snickered, "There are great pastors in this world, but people like you only focus on the bad ones. Those that take money from people have received their reward on Earth. Real Christians know their reward is in Heaven."

Tony walked into the room and pushed Toby to the floor. Blade laughed, "Well, look who has decided to join us. Mister Hackerman himself. I got plans for you before I kill you."

Toby said, "I'm not doing anything for you."

"People always say that until they realize they don't have a choice." Blade got in Toby's face, "You'll do what I ask, or you'll die."

"I'd rather die."

"How about your grandmother? Would you rather watch her die? I'll kill all your people first, then you." Toby did not respond. "I thought you'd change your mind. Now the only person we need at this party is Officer Blaylock, and that coward Blake. Tony…"

"Yes, sir."

"I'll be in the den. Let me know when they arrive."

"Yes, sir." Blade left the room. Tony walked up to Twanda and slapped her hard in the face. "You killed my brother, and that's something I won't ever forget. I'm going to enjoy watching you die."

Twanda did not answer. She spit the blood to the floor. Blade's people wanted her dead. All her life, she was loved by many. No one wanted her dead, but in the last couple of days, it seemed everyone wanted her dead. She looked at Toby and felt bad as she dragged him into her situation.

Tony and Kenyon walked out of the room. Twanda cursed herself for visions of killing Tony, too. Her faith had been placed on a shelf as she tried to get through this valley experience of her life. She asked Toby, "Are you okay?"

"Yeah, I'm a bit bruised, but I'm okay. What do you think he wants from me?"

Twanda popped her lips, "No one knew how talented a hacker you were until I came into your life. Now I've exposed you to Blade, and he's going to use your talent for evil. I'm so sorry, Toby."

"Nothing for you to be sorry about. So you found out your boyfriend is working for Blade. I tried to tell you that before you went to the meet, but you didn't hear me screaming into the phone."

"Yeah, I didn't, but he got himself into a jam taking money from Blade. Of course, Blade lied to him, and now he's going to use his business to sell his drugs."

"That's so Blade-like."

"Yes, it is. We have to keep our eyes open for a way out. Sometimes the best plan won't materialize until the last minute."

"I'll be ready. Maybe we should have a code or something. A word that once said we know to act."

"You watch too much television, Toby. Just watch me. You'll know."

Toby chuckled, "You know, if I didn't know you, I would think you were a full-fledged FBI agent now."

"I learned a lot in college."

Toby laughed, "So I see. I will rely on you, my friend, but any chance I get to get on a computer, I will take advantage of it. Blade should know that you should never give a hacker a computer."

"Just be careful. Sounds like I heard a car."

"I heard it too. Maybe it's Blaylock."

"We might be able to turn them against each other. Remember, watch me."

"Will do."

Twanda's mind retreated into thought. Different plans rushed across her mind, but the most prevalent thoughts were on her father. She wished she could bury him. She bowed her head and prayed to her Lord and Savior. *"Dear Heavenly Father, the hour is now. I need you to intervene in this situation. So many of my enemies want me dead, but I know you can protect me. My friend Toby has strayed off the path but, Lord, protect him anyway. Show him your power. Father, cleanse my heart of the thoughts that I have had of killing Blade and Tony. It is not my place to judge them. Allow me to get out of this situation safely to say goodbye to my father. In your awesome son, Jesus' name... Amen."*

Officer Blaylock and Officer Blake walked into the damp room. She looked at Toby, then Twanda and said, "Girl, you have been trouble for all of us. I think you would have been a great law enforcement officer."

"I can't believe I admired you."

"There was a time when I should have been admired. That time has passed and now I have to do what I can to protect myself. Unfortunately for you, that means I can't have you testifying about my involvement with Blade." Twanda looked away with disgust.

Blade, Tony, and Kenyon walked into the room. Blade said, "It seems we're all here. Where's the evidence?"

Officer Blake replied, "I have it. Where's the money?" Blade motioned to Tony and Tony opened a suitcase displaying the money. Officer Blake continued, "Now, that's what I'm talking about. Slide the cash over to me and I'll email you the file when we're safe in our car."

Blade chuckled, "Am I a fool? You're not getting out of here with my money if I don't get that file."

Blake replied, "Then we have an issue. I don't trust you and you don't trust me. What do we do?"

Twanda readied herself to make a move. Something was going to happen. Neither side trusted the other, and this presented a window of opportunity for her. Officer Blaylock pulled her weapon. Tony went for his weapon and she shot him in the shoulder. Officer Blaylock said, "Now, hand over the money, and like Blake said, we'll give you the file when we get to the car."

Blade rolled his eyes at both officers. "This is a mistake, Blaylock."

"Mistake or not, we need to get out of here. I'm sure you're planning to kill us all."

Blade did not respond. Twanda noticed Tony's gun was near Toby. She starred at him, hoping he would get the message to grab the gun. Twanda was going to jump Officer Blaylock. If Toby gets the message, she could create enough commotion that they might get away.

Twanda counted down silently with her lips, *"Three, two, one…"* She darted to Officer Blaylock, catching her off guard. Twanda knocked her to the ground and grabbed her gun. Toby grabbed Tony's gun. Blake fired at Blade and Tony. Blade fired back.

Blade rushed out of the room. Officer Blake grabbed the bag of money and kept shooting at Toby and Twanda. Twanda said, "We need to get that file."

Toby said, "Don't worry. That's not the only file."

Blake's shot hit Twanda. She spun around and fell to the ground. Toby fired back at him and hit him in the stomach. He went to his knees. Officer

Blaylock attempted to grab the money, but Toby's shots moved her away.

Officer Blaylock ran out of the room, leaving the bags of money with Toby. He knelt by Twanda. "Are you okay?"

"Yeah, I don't think it's that bad."

"Here, let me wrap it in this." Toby wrapped her arm up. "Let's get out of here."

Chapter 11

Twanda watched the news reporter tell the world about Officer Blake's death. The reporter stood in front of police headquarters with the chief of police, the mayor, and Officer Blaylock. Two large monitors were on either side of the group. It was clear they wanted a large crowd with the widest dissemination of coverage for this story.

Again, they pinned Officer Blake's murder on her because Officer Blaylock was there to tell the story. However, this time, Twanda had friends in place.

Officer Blaylock took the microphone. Her face was plastered on both monitors. She said, "The last three days, Twanda Cousins has been on a murder spree. She started this spree by killing Officer Diego Ramirez and ended with the murder of another great officer and friend of mine Office Jeffrey R. Blake. Her actions will not go…"

Twanda walked out of the shadows to a spot where she could be seen by Officer Blaylock. Officer Blaylock shouted, "Arrest her!"

Officers from every direction pointed their weapons at Twanda. Twanda rose her hands over her head. Officer Blaylock said, "Twanda Cousins, your reign of murder is over. You will go to prison for life for the murders of Officer Ramirez and Office Blake." Twanda smiled. Officer Blaylock continued, "Look at her. She's a narcissist smiling at the loss of police lives."

Twanda looked up at the monitor. It started, "Hi my name is Twanda Cousins. I'm sure you recognize me because my face has been plastered on your television sets everywhere. However, what you don't know is that I did not kill Officer Ramirez. Blade killed him with the knowledge of Officer Blaylock." The video of Twanda faded out and the body cam video of Blade and Officer Blaylock started. The officers who once held their weapons at Twanda begin to drop their weapons and stare at Officer Blaylock.

Officer Blaylock took a few steps away from the podium, but she could not escape the officers. The chief of police ordered her arrest. Sergeant Benson walked up to Twanda, "Miss Cousins, I couldn't believe you killed Diego. I'm glad I was right. You're free to go."

"What about Blade?"

"We have a warrant out of his arrest. It's a matter of time before we get him."

"What's going to happen to Officer Blaylock?"

"I imagine she's going to prison for a long time. She's an accessory after the fact to murder." He took a deep breath. "Who knows what else we'll discover when all of this is over."

"Officer Blake was killed in a shootout. It's all in this statement."

Sergeant Benson grinned, "You came prepared."

"I did, but I had some friends." She turned and walked away. After a few feet away, she dialed the number. "Hey, this is Twanda. Is he there?"

"Yes, we have him. Are you on the way?"

"I am." Twanda hung up, jumped in her car and headed to the meet. It had been a long time since she would get the satisfaction she looked for. She arrived at the house and walked inside. She smiled at the sight she only imagined over the prior three days. "This is a nice sight to see."

"You can't hold me here."

"Oh, why? Because you're the big bad Blade? Not anymore, my friend. You're done in East City. No one is afraid of you anymore."

Toby asked, "Are you really going to kill him?"

"I want to, but my Father in Heaven would not be proud. I called Sergeant Benson while I was on the way here. They'll come and get him."

"Whew, just when I was starting to believe in God again, you gave me doubts. I'm glad you came around."

"I'm headed to do some good in the world." Twanda walked out of the room. Before she left, she turned to Blade and said, "Diego was a good man. I hope they fry you for what you did to him." Blade sneered. Twanda left. Her drive through the city was peaceful. She rolled her window down and let the breeze rush to her pretty face.

Twanda was free, and no one chased her any longer. She pulled up in front of the quaint home. *"There's no way he was on the take."* She watched the two little boys playing in front and smiled. Twanda grabbed the suitcase from the seat of the car and headed to the front door. She was met by a beautiful Hispanic woman. She thought, *"Diego had great taste."* Twanda reached out her hand, "Hi, I'm Twanda Cousins and I knew your husband."

She replied, "I'm Valentina and I know who you are. For days, I hated you and I hoped they would catch you and kill you. I'm sorry for that."

"Hey, I get it. The police made it seem to everyone that I killed Diego, but I could never have done that. I only knew him for a few hours, but he was a great officer."

"The police won't give me any money to bury him. They say they are investigating the accusations that he was dirty. I said, we're living paycheck-to-paycheck. How could he be dirty."

"Diego's name will be cleared. In the meantime, here's something to help you bury him and take care of your boys."

Valentina opened the briefcase and gasped, "My Lord… I can't take this? They will surely think Diego was dirty."

"No, they won't. I've already informed them I have the money and I'm giving half of it to you. The other half will go to Southeast to help build up the community and get rid of people like Blade. They didn't argue because of all the Hell they put me through."

"Thank you, Twanda."

Twanda hugged Valentina. "Diego loved those boys. This money will give them a chance."

Something caught Twanda's attention. "What is that smell?"

Valentina smiled, "That's my homemade empanadas. Would you like some?"

"Sure." They sat down with the boys and engaged in a meal. For the first time in days, Twanda's heart was at peace.

Two Days Later

Twanda stood by the gravesite, burying her father. The last of her family now laid peacefully at rest. The next day, she would drive to Quantico and begin her training as an FBI agent. Through it all, she realized she could do more good by becoming a good agent than anything else. Joining her at her side was Kenyon.

"I'm really sorry about everything, Twanda."

Anger welled up in her spirit, but she quashed it and remained peaceful and focused. She turned to him and plastered a smiled on her face, hoping it did not give off the air that it was fake. Despite it all, she did not want to hurt his feelings. "I'm sorry too, Kenyon. We could have had a wonderful life together."

"We still can."

She popped her lips, "No, we can't. I can't be with a man who wouldn't be proud to honor his vow of chastity to his friends. But the real deal breaker was taking money from Blade, then turning on me. You were ready to see me die. A man that loves me would never allow someone to kill me."

"I can do better. Just give me one more chance."

She plastered her fake smile again, "I can't." She patted him on the shoulder and walked away, leaving Kenyon standing by the grave. Her valley experience with Blade and the criminal underworld changed a lot about her, but in the end, it strengthened her faith and love for God.

Author Bio

Gerald C. Anderson, Sr. was born and raised in Tampa, Florida. He spent most of his childhood life growing up in the Belmont Heights area of Tampa.

In 1980, Gerald graduated from C. Leon King Senior High School in Temple Terrace, Florida. Following graduation, he enlisted in the United States Air Force.

Air Force Life

In his service career, Gerald traveled the world with assignments to California (twice), Florida, Kansas, Maryland, West Germany, and Korea. Upon his last assignment in Maryland and after retirement from the Air Force, Gerald began working in the United States Federal Government's Department of Energy. In 2003, he moved to the Internal Revenue

Service, and in 2007 he joined the Department of Education.

Education

In 2005, Gerald got his Bachelor of Science degree in Computer Information Systems from Strayer University, and in 2008 he received his Master of Administration degree in Criminal Justice Administration from the University of Cincinnati (UC).

Published Books

We Come in Peace

27 Hours (What Would You Do If You Faced the End?)

Standing Firm (One Family's Fight Against Domestic Violence)

Secrets (Silent Screams in The Dark)

The Last Song

The Lawyer

Saved

The Room

Are You Innocent?

The Compendium Series

Weight Loss

Warlord

The Last Honorable Man

The Dream

The Death Knights

Twins

A Saved Man

In 1992, Gerald turned his life over to Jesus Christ and a life with Christ at the head. He is a musician in church. He continues to live in Maryland with his son.

Thank You!

I would like to take this opportunity to thank you for reading my novella. "The Ride Along" was written to entertain my Christian fanbase. I hope I accomplished this goal, and you have enjoyed the story and maybe learned something from it.

Please consider reading my previous novels and short stories listed at the front of this novel. I also manage a Christian lifestyle magazine, "The Lyfe Magazine" (www.thelyfemagazine.com).

Lastly, if you enjoyed this novella, please go to Amazon and write me a review. Reviews help move novels, novellas and short stories on Amazon so that other potential readers can find it.

Thank you so much and always have a blessed day!

Gerald C. Anderson, Sr.

www.ingramcontent.com/pod-product-compliance
Lightning Source LLC
Chambersburg PA
CBHW021341290326
41933CB00037B/314